# Internet Law

## Key Statutes

2022

Third Edition

ANUPAM CHANDER

Scott K. Ginsburg Professor
of Law and Technology
Georgetown University Law Center

D1157812

Many thanks to Shiwen Cai, Maya Krishnan, and Ryan Whittington for assistance.

Internet Law: Key Statutes (3rd edition)

Copyright © 2022 Anupam Chander

ISBN: 9798792551411

Cover image by Garry Knight via Flickr

## TABLE OF CONTENTS

# Copyright

# DMCA Title I: Circumvention of Copyright Protection Systems
## *17 USC § 1201 et seq.*

### 17 U.S.C. §1201

(a)    (1) Violations regarding circumvention of technological measures—

(A) No person shall circumvent a technological measure that effectively controls access to a work protected under this title. The prohibition contained in the preceding sentence shall take effect at the end of the 2-year period beginning on the date of the enactment of this chapter [17 U.S.C.A. § 1201 et seq.].

(B) The prohibition contained in subparagraph (A) shall not apply to persons who are users of a copyrighted work which is in a particular class of works, if such persons are, or are likely to be in the succeeding 3-year period, adversely affected by virtue of such prohibition in their ability to make noninfringing uses of that particular class of works under this title, as determined under subparagraph (C).

(C) During the 2-year period described in subparagraph (A), and during each succeeding 3-year period, the Librarian of Congress, upon the recommendation of the Register of Copyrights, who shall consult with the Assistant Secretary for Communications and Information of the Department of Commerce and report and comment on his or her views in making such recommendation, shall make the determination in a rulemaking proceeding for purposes of subparagraph (B) of whether persons who are users of a copyrighted work are, or are likely to be in the succeeding 3-year period, adversely affected by the prohibition under subparagraph (A) in their ability to make noninfringing uses under this title of a particular class of copyrighted works. In conducting such rulemaking, the Librarian shall examine—

(i) the availability for use of copyrighted works;

(ii) the availability for use of works for nonprofit archival, preservation, and educational purposes;

(iii) the impact that the prohibition on the circumvention of technological measures applied to copyrighted works has on criticism, comment, news reporting, teaching, scholarship, or research;

(iv) the effect of circumvention of technological measures on the market for or value of copyrighted works; and

(v) such other factors as the Librarian considers appropriate.

(D) The Librarian shall publish any class of copyrighted works for which the Librarian has determined, pursuant to the rulemaking conducted under subparagraph (C), that noninfringing uses by persons who are users of a copyrighted work are, or are likely to be, adversely affected, and the prohibition contained in subparagraph (A) shall not apply to such users with respect to such class of works for the ensuing 3-year period.

(E) Neither the exception under subparagraph (B) from the applicability of the prohibition contained in subparagraph (A), nor any determination made in a rulemaking conducted under subparagraph (C), may be used as a defense in any action to enforce any provision of this title other than this paragraph.

(2) No person shall manufacture, import, offer to the public, provide, or otherwise traffic in any technology, product, service, device, component, or part thereof, that—

(A) is primarily designed or produced for the purpose of circumventing a technological measure that effectively controls access to a work protected under this title;

(B) has only limited commercially significant purpose or use other than to circumvent a technological measure that effectively controls access to a work protected under this title [17 U.S.C.A. § 1 et seq.]; or

(C) is marketed by that person or another acting in concert with that person with that person's knowledge for use in circumventing a technological measure that effectively controls access to a work protected under this title.

(3) As used in this subsection—

(A) to "circumvent a technological measure" means to descramble a scrambled work, to decrypt an encrypted work, or otherwise to avoid, bypass, remove, deactivate, or impair a technological measure, without the authority of the copyright owner; and

(B) a technological measure "effectively controls access to a work" if the measure, in the ordinary course of its operation, requires the application of information, or a process or a treatment, with the authority of the copyright owner, to gain access to the work.

(b) Additional violations.—

(1) No person shall manufacture, import, offer to the public, provide, or otherwise traffic in any technology, product, service, device, component, or part thereof, that—

(A) is primarily designed or produced for the purpose of circumventing protection afforded by a technological measure that effectively protects a right of a copyright owner under this title [17 U.S.C.A. § 1 et seq.] in a work or a portion thereof;

(B) has only limited commercially significant purpose or use other than to circumvent protection afforded by a technological measure that effectively protects a right of a copyright owner under this title in a work or a portion thereof; or

(C) is marketed by that person or another acting in concert with that person with that person's knowledge for use in circumventing protection afforded by a technological measure that effectively protects a right of a copyright owner under this title in a work or a portion thereof.

(2) As used in this subsection—

(A) to "circumvent protection afforded by a technological measure" means avoiding, bypassing, removing, deactivating, or otherwise impairing a technological measure; and

(B) a technological measure 'effectively protects a right of a copyright owner under this title' if the measure, in the ordinary course of its operation, prevents, restricts, or otherwise limits the exercise of a right of a copyright owner under this title.

(c) Other rights, etc., not affected.—

(1) Nothing in this section shall affect rights, remedies, limitations, or defenses to copyright infringement, including fair use, under this title [17 U.S.C.A. § 1 et seq.].

(2) "Nothing in this section shall enlarge or diminish vicarious or contributory liability for copyright infringement in connection with any technology, product, service, device, component, or part thereof."

(3) Nothing in this section shall require that the design of, or design and selection of parts and components for, a consumer electronics, telecommunications, or computing product provide for a response to any particular technological measure, so long as such part or component, or the product in which such part or component is integrated, does not otherwise fall within the prohibitions of subsection (a)(2) or (b)(1).

(4) Nothing in this section shall enlarge or diminish any rights of free speech or the press for activities using consumer electronics, telecommunications, or computing products. ***

(d) Exemption for nonprofit libraries, archives, and educational institutions.—

(1) A nonprofit library, archives, or educational institution which gains access to a commercially exploited copyrighted work solely in order to make a good faith determination of whether to acquire a copy of that work for the sole purpose of engaging in conduct permitted under this title [17 U.S.C.A. § 1 et seq.] shall not be in violation of subsection (a)(1)(A). A copy of a work to which access has been gained under this paragraph—

(A) may not be retained longer than necessary to make such good faith determination; and

(B) may not be used for any other purpose.

(2) The exemption made available under paragraph (1) shall only apply with respect to a work when an identical copy of that work is not reasonably available in another form.

(3) A nonprofit library, archives, or educational institution that willfully for the purpose of commercial advantage or financial gain violates paragraph (1)--

(A) shall, for the first offense, be subject to the civil remedies under section 1203; and

(B) shall, for repeated or subsequent offenses, in addition to the civil remedies under section 1203, forfeit the exemption provided under paragraph (1).

(4) This subsection may not be used as a defense to a claim under subsection (a)(2) or (b), nor may this subsection permit a nonprofit library, archives, or educational institution to manufacture, import, offer to the public, provide, or otherwise traffic in any technology, product, service, component, or part thereof, which circumvents a technological measure.

(5) In order for a library or archives to qualify for the exemption under this subsection, the collections of that library or archives shall be—

(A) open to the public; or

(B) available not only to researchers affiliated with the library or archives or with the institution of which it is a part, but also to other persons doing research in a specialized field.

(e) Law enforcement, intelligence, and other government activities.—This section does not prohibit any lawfully authorized investigative, protective, information security, or intelligence activity of an officer, agent, or employee of the United States, a State, or a political subdivision of a State, or a person acting pursuant to a contract with the United States, a State, or a political subdivision of a State. For purposes of this subsection, the term "information security" means activities carried out in order to identify and address the vulnerabilities of a government computer, computer system, or computer network.

(f) Reverse engineering.—

(1) Notwithstanding the provisions of subsection (a)(1)(A), a person who has lawfully obtained the right to use a copy of a computer program may circumvent a technological measure that effectively controls access to a particular portion of that program for the sole purpose of identifying and analyzing those elements of the program that are necessary to achieve interoperability of an independently created computer program with other programs, and that have not previously been readily available to the person engaging in the circumvention, to the extent any such acts of identification and analysis do not constitute infringement under this title [17 U.S.C.A. § 1 et seq.].

(2) Notwithstanding the provisions of subsections (a)(2) and (b), a person may develop and employ technological means to circumvent a technological measure, or to circumvent protection afforded by a technological measure, in order to enable the identification and analysis under paragraph (1), or for the purpose of enabling interoperability of an independently created computer program with other programs, if such means are necessary to achieve such interoperability, to the extent that doing so does not constitute infringement under this title [17 U.S.C.A. § 1 et seq.].

(3) The information acquired through the acts permitted under paragraph (1), and the means permitted under paragraph (2), may be made available to others if the person referred to in paragraph (1) or (2), as the case may be, provides such information or means solely for the purpose of enabling interoperability of an independently created computer program with other programs, and to the extent that doing so does not constitute infringement under this title [17 U.S.C.A. § 1 et seq.] or violate applicable law other than this section.

(4) For purposes of this subsection, the term "interoperability" means the ability of computer programs to exchange information, and of such programs mutually to use the information which has been exchanged.

* * *

(h) Exceptions regarding minors.—In applying subsection (a) to a component or part, the court may consider the necessity for its intended and actual incorporation in a technology, product, service, or device, which—

(1) does not itself violate the provisions of this title [17 U.S.C.A. § 1 et seq.]; and

(2) has the sole purpose to prevent the access of minors to material on the Internet.

* * *

(j) Security testing.

> (1) Definition. For purposes of this subsection, the term "security testing" means accessing a computer, computer system, or computer network, solely for the purpose of good faith testing, investigating, or correcting, a security flaw or vulnerability, with the authorization of the owner or operator of such computer, computer system, or computer network...

## 17 U.S.C. §1203

(a) Civil actions. Any person injured by a violation of section 1201 or 1202 may bring a civil action in an appropriate United States district court for such violation.

(b) Powers of the court. In an action brought under subsection (a), the court—

> (1) may grant temporary and permanent injunctions on such terms as it deems reasonable to prevent or restrain a violation, but in no event shall impose a prior restraint on free speech or the press protected under the 1st amendment to the Constitution;

> (2) at any time while an action is pending, may order the impounding, on such terms as it deems reasonable, of any device or product that is in the custody or control of the alleged violator and that the court has reasonable cause to believe was involved in a violation;

> (3) may award damages under subsection (C);

> (4) in its discretion may allow the recovery of costs by or against any party other than the United States or an officer thereof;

> (5) in its discretion may award reasonable attorney's fees to the prevailing party; and

> (6) may, as part of a final judgment or decree finding a violation, order the remedial modification or the destruction of any device or product involved in the violation that is in the custody or control of the violator or has been impounded under paragraph (2).

(c) Award of damages.

> (1) In general. Except as otherwise provided in this title, a person committing a violation of section 1201 or 1202 is liable for either—

>> (A) the actual damages and any additional profits of the violator, as provided in paragraph (2), or

>> (B) statutory damages, as provided in paragraph (3).

> (2) Actual damages. The court shall award to the complaining party the actual damages suffered by the party as a result of the violation, and any profits of the violator that are attributable to the violation and are not taken into account in computing the actual damages, if the complaining party elects such damages at any time before final judgment is entered.

> (3) Statutory damages.

(A) At any time before final judgment is entered, a complaining party may elect to recover an award of statutory damages for each violation of section 1201 in the sum of not less than $200 or more than $2,500 per act of circumvention, device, product, component, offer, or performance of service, as the court considers just.

(B) At any time before final judgment is entered, a complaining party may elect to recover an award of statutory damages for each violation of section 1202 in the sum of not less than $2,500 or more than $25,000.

(4) Repeated violations. In any case in which the injured party sustains the burden of proving, and the court finds, that a person has violated section 1201 or 1202 within 3 years after a final judgment was entered against the person for another such violation, the court may increase the award of damages up to triple the amount that would otherwise be awarded, as the court considers just.

(5) Innocent violations.

(A) In general. The court in its discretion may reduce or remit the total award of damages in any case in which the violator sustains the burden of proving, and the court finds, that the violator was not aware and had no reason to believe that its acts constituted a violation.

(B) Nonprofit library, archives, educational institutions, or public broadcasting entities.

(i) Definition. In this subparagraph, the term "public broadcasting entity" has the meaning given such term under section 118(g).

(ii) In general. In the case of a nonprofit library, archives, educational institution, or public broadcasting entity, the court shall remit damages in any case in which the library, archives, educational institution, or public broadcasting entity sustains the burden of proving, and the court finds, that the library, archives, educational institution, or public broadcasting entity was not aware and had no reason to believe that its acts constituted a violation.

### 17 U.S.C. §1204

(a) In general. Any person who violates section 1201 or 1202 willfully and for purposes of commercial advantage or private financial gain—

(1) shall be fined not more than $500,000 or imprisoned for not more than 5 years, or both, for the first offense; and

(2) shall be fined not more than $1,000,000 or imprisoned for not more than 10 years, or both, for any subsequent offense.

(b) Limitation for nonprofit library, archives, educational institution, or public broadcasting entity.—Subsection (a) shall not apply to a nonprofit library, archives, educational institution, or public broadcasting entity (as defined under section 118(g).

(c) Statute of limitations. No criminal proceeding shall be brought under this section unless such proceeding is commenced within 5 years after the cause of action arose.

## COPYRIGHT ACT: LIMITATIONS ON EXCLUSIVE USE: FAIR USE
### *17 USC § 107*

Notwithstanding the provisions of sections 106 and 106A, the fair use of a copyrighted work, including such use by reproduction in copies or phonorecords or by any other means specified by that section, for purposes such as criticism, comment, news reporting, teaching (including multiple copies for classroom use), scholarship, or research, is not an infringement of copyright. In determining whether the use made of a work in any particular case is a fair use the factors to be considered shall include—

(1) the purpose and character of the use, including whether such use is of a commercial nature or is for nonprofit educational purposes;

(2) the nature of the copyrighted work;

(3) the amount and substantiality of the portion used in relation to the copyrighted work as a whole; and

(4) the effect of the use upon the potential market for or value of the copyrighted work.

# DMCA Title II: Online Copyright Infringement Limitation Act, *17 USC § 512*

(a) Transitory digital network communications -- A service provider shall not be liable for monetary relief, or, except as provided in subsection (j), for injunctive or other equitable relief, for infringement of copyright by reason of the provider's transmitting, routing, or providing connections for, material through a system or network controlled or operated by or for the service provider, or by reason of the intermediate and transient storage of that material in the course of such transmitting, routing, or providing connections, if

> (1) the transmission of the material was initiated by or at the direction of a person other than the service provider;

> (2) the transmission, routing, provision of connections, or storage is carried out through an automatic technical process without selection of the material by the service provider;

> (3) the service provider does not select the recipients of the material except as an automatic response to the request of another person;

> (4) no copy of the material made by the service provider in the course of such intermediate or transient storage is maintained on the system or network in a manner ordinarily accessible to anyone other than anticipated recipients, and no such copy is maintained on the system or network in a manner ordinarily accessible to such anticipated recipients for a longer period than is reasonably necessary for the transmission, routing, or provision of connections; and

> (5) the material is transmitted through the system or network without modification of its content.

(b) System caching.

> (1) Limitation on liability. A service provider shall not be liable for monetary relief, or, except as provided in subsection (j), for injunctive or other equitable relief, for infringement of copyright by reason of the intermediate and temporary storage of material on a system or network controlled or operated by or for the service provider in a case in which

>> (A) the material is made available online by a person other than the service provider;

>> (B) the material is transmitted from the person described in subparagraph (A) through the system or network to a person other than the person described in subparagraph (A) at the direction of that other person; and

>> (C) the storage is carried out through an automatic technical process for the purpose of making the material available to of the system or network who, after the material is transmitted as described in subparagraph (B), request access to the material from the person described in subparagraph (A); if the conditions set forth in paragraph (2) are met.

> (2) Conditions. The conditions referred to in paragraph (1) are that

(A) the material described in paragraph (1) is transmitted to the subsequent users described in paragraph (1)(C) without modification to its content from the manner in which the material was transmitted from the person described in paragraph (1)(A);

(B) the service provider described in paragraph (1) complies with rules concerning the refreshing, reloading, or other updating of the material when specified by the person making the material available online in accordance with a generally accepted industry standard data communications protocol for the system or network through which that person makes the material available, except that this subparagraph applies only if those rules are not used by the person described in paragraph (1)(A) to prevent or unreasonably impair the intermediate storage to which this subsection applies;

(C) the service provider does not interfere with the ability of technology associated with the material to return to the person described in paragraph (1)(A) the information that would have been available to that person if the material had been obtained by the subsequent users described in paragraph (1)(C) directly from that person, except that this subparagraph applies only if that technology

(i) does not significantly interfere with the performance of the provider's system or network or with the intermediate storage of the material;

(ii) is consistent with generally accepted industry standard communications protocols; and

(iii) does not extract information from the provider's system or network other than the information that would have been available to the person described in paragraph (1)(A) if the subsequent users had gained access to the material directly from that person;

(D) if the person described in paragraph (1)(A) has in effect a condition that a person must meet prior to having access to the material, such as a condition based on payment of a fee or provision of a password or other information, the service provider permits access to the stored material in significant part only to users of its system or network that have met those conditions and only in accordance with those conditions; and

(E) if the person described in paragraph (1)(A) makes that material available online without the authorization of the copyright owner of the material, the service provider responds expeditiously to remove, or disable access to, the material that is claimed to be infringing upon notification of claimed infringement as described in subsection (c)(3), except that this subparagraph applies only if

(i) the material has previously been removed from the originating site or access to it has been disabled, or a court has ordered that the material be removed from the originating site or that access to the material on the originating site be disabled; and

(ii) the party giving the notification includes in the notification a statement confirming that the material has been removed from the originating site or access to it has been disabled or that a court has ordered that the material be removed from the originating site or that access to the material on the originating site be disabled.

(c) Information residing on systems or networks at direction of users.

(1) In general. A service provider shall not be liable for monetary relief, or, except as provided in subsection (j), for injunctive or other equitable relief, for infringement of copyright by reason of the storage at the direction of a user of material that resides on a system or network controlled or operated by or for the service provider, if the service provider

(A)     (i) does not have actual knowledge that the material or an activity using the material on the system or network is infringing;

(ii) in the absence of such actual knowledge, is not aware of facts or circumstances from which infringing activity is apparent; or

(iii) upon obtaining such knowledge or awareness, acts expeditiously to remove, or disable access to, the material;

(B) does not receive a financial benefit directly attributable to the infringing activity, in a case in which the service provider has the right and ability to control such activity; and

(C) upon notification of claimed infringement as described in paragraph (3), responds expeditiously to remove, or disable access to, the material that is claimed to be infringing or to be the subject of infringing activity.

(2) Designated agent. The limitations on liability established in this subsection apply to a service provider only if the service provider has designated an agent to receive notifications of claimed infringement described in paragraph (3), by making available through its service, including on its website in a location accessible to the public, and by providing to the Copyright Office, substantially the following information:

(A) the name, address, phone number, and electronic mail address of the agent.

(B) other contact information which the Register of Copyrights may deem appropriate.

The Register of Copyrights shall maintain a current directory of agents available to the public for inspection, including through the Internet, in both electronic and hard copy formats, and may require payment of a fee by service providers to cover the costs of maintaining the directory.

(3) Elements of notification

(A) To be effective under this subsection, a notification of claimed infringement must be a written communication provided to the designated agent of a service provider that includes substantially the following:

(i) A physical or electronic signature of a person authorized to act on behalf of the owner of an exclusive right that is allegedly infringed.

(ii) Identification of the copyrighted work claimed to have been infringed, or, if multiple copyrighted works at a single online site are covered by a single notification, a representative list of such works at that site.

(iii) Identification of the material that is claimed to be infringing or to be the subject of infringing activity and that is to be removed or access to which is to be disabled, and information reasonably sufficient to permit the service provider to locate the material.

(iv) Information reasonably sufficient to permit the service provider to contact the complaining party, such as an address, telephone number, and, if available, an electronic mail address at which the complaining party may be contacted.

(v) A statement that the complaining party has a good faith belief that use of the material in the manner complained of is not authorized by the copyright owner, its agent, or the law.

(vi) A statement that the information in the notification is accurate, and under penalty of perjury, that the complaining party is authorized to act on behalf of the owner of an exclusive right that is allegedly infringed.

(B)     (i) Subject to clause (ii), a notification from a copyright owner or from a person authorized to act on behalf of the copyright owner that fails to comply substantially with the provisions of subparagraph (A) shall not be considered under paragraph (1)(A) in determining whether a service provider has actual knowledge or is aware of facts or circumstances from which infringing activity is apparent.

(ii) In a case in which the notification that is provided to the service provider's designated agent fails to comply substantially with all the provisions of subparagraph (A) but substantially complies with clauses (ii), (iii), and (iv) of subparagraph (A), clause (i) of this subparagraph applies only if the service provider promptly attempts to contact the person making the notification or takes other reasonable steps to assist in the receipt of notification that substantially complies with all the provisions of subparagraph (A).

(d) Information location tools. A service provider shall not be liable for monetary relief, or, except as provided in subsection (j), for injunctive or other equitable relief, for infringement of copyright by reason of the provider referring or linking users to an online location containing infringing material or infringing activity, by using information location tools, including a directory, index, reference, pointer, or hypertext link, if the service provider

(1)     (A) does not have actual knowledge that the material or activity is infringing;

(B) in the absence of such actual knowledge, is not aware of facts or circumstances from which infringing activity is apparent; or

(C) upon obtaining such knowledge or awareness, acts expeditiously to remove, or disable access to, the material;

(2) does not receive a financial benefit directly attributable to the infringing activity, in a case in which the service provider has the right and ability to control such activity; and

(3) upon notification of claimed infringement as described in subsection (C)(3), responds expeditiously to remove, or disable access to, the material that is claimed to be infringing or to be the subject of infringing activity, except that, for purposes of this paragraph, the information described in subsection (C)(3)(A)(iii) shall be identification of the reference or link, to material or activity claimed to be infringing, that is to be removed or access to which is to be disabled, and information reasonably sufficient to permit the service provider to locate that reference or link.

(e) Limitation on liability of nonprofit educational institutions

(1) When a public or other nonprofit institution of higher education is a service provider, and when a faculty member or graduate student who is an employee of such institution is performing a teaching or research function, for the purposes of subsections (a) and (b) such faculty member or graduate student shall be considered to be a person other than the institution, and for the purposes of subsections (c) and (d) such faculty member's or graduate student's knowledge or awareness of his or her infringing activities shall not be attributed to the institution, if

(A) such faculty member's or graduate student's infringing activities do not involve the provision of online access to instructional materials that are or were required or recommended, within the preceding 3-year period, for a course taught at the institution by such faculty member or graduate student;

(B) the institution has not, within the preceding 3-year period, received more than two notifications described in subsection (c)(3) of claimed infringement by such faculty member or graduate student, and such notifications of claimed infringement were not actionable under subsection (f); and

(C) the institution provides to all users of its system or network informational materials that accurately describe, and promote compliance with, the laws of the United States relating to copyright.

(2) For the purposes of this subsection, the limitations on injunctive relief contained in subsections (j)(2) and (j)(3), but not those in (j)(1), shall apply.

(f) Misrepresentations. Any person who knowingly materially misrepresents under this section

(1) that material or activity is infringing, or

(2) that material or activity was removed or disabled by mistake or misidentification,

shall be liable for any damages, including costs and attorneys" fees, incurred by the alleged infringer, by any copyright owner or copyright owner's authorized licensee, or by a service provider, who is injured by such misrepresentation, as the result of the service provider relying upon such misrepresentation in removing or disabling access to the material or activity claimed to be infringing, or in replacing the removed material or ceasing to disable access to it

(g) Replacement of removed or disabled material and limitation on other liability

(1) No liability for taking down generally. Subject to paragraph (2), a service provider shall not be liable to any person for any claim based on the service provider's good faith disabling of access to, or removal of, material or activity claimed to be infringing or based on facts or circumstances from which infringing activity is apparent, regardless of whether the material or activity is ultimately determined to be infringing.

(2) Exception. Paragraph (1) shall not apply with respect to material residing at the direction of a subscriber of the service provider on a system or network controlled or operated by or for the service provider that is removed, or to which access is disabled by the service provider, pursuant to a notice provided under subsection (C)(1)(C), unless the service provider

> (A) takes reasonable steps promptly to notify the subscriber that it has removed or disabled access to the material;

> (B) upon receipt of a counter notification described in paragraph (3), promptly provides the person who provided the notification under subsection (c)(1)(C) with a copy of the counter notification, and informs that person that it will replace the removed material or cease disabling access to it in 10 business days; and

> (C) replaces the removed material and ceases disabling access to it not less than 10, nor more than 14, business days following receipt of the counter notice, unless its designated agent first receives notice from the person who submitted the notification under subsection (C)(1)(C) that such person has filed an action seeking a court order to restrain the subscriber from engaging in infringing activity relating to the material on the service provider's system or network.

(3) Contents of counter notification .To be effective under this subsection, a counter notification must be a written communication provided to the service provider's designated agent that includes substantially the following:

> (A) A physical or electronic signature of the subscriber.

> (B) Identification of the material that has been removed or to which access has been disabled and the location at which the material appeared before it was removed or access to it was disabled.

> (C) A statement under penalty of perjury that the subscriber has a good faith belief that the material was removed or disabled as a result of mistake or misidentification of the material to be removed or disabled.

> (D) The subscriber's name, address, and telephone number, and a statement that the subscriber consents to the jurisdiction of Federal District Court for the judicial district in which the address is located, or if the subscriber's address is outside of the United States, for any judicial district in which the service provider may be found, and that the subscriber will accept service of process from the person who provided notification under subsection (C)(1)(C) or an agent of such person.

(4) Limitation on other liability. A service provider's compliance with paragraph (2) shall not subject the service provider to liability for copyright infringement with respect to the material identified in the notice provided under subsection (C)(1)(C).

(h) Subpoena to identify infringer.

(1) Request. A copyright owner or a person authorized to act on the owner's behalf may request the clerk of any United States district court to issue a subpoena to a service provider for identification of an alleged infringer in accordance with this subsection.

(2) Contents of request. The request may be made by filing with the clerk

(A) a copy of a notification described in subsection (c)(3)(A);

(B) a proposed subpoena; and

(C) a sworn declaration to the effect that the purpose for which the subpoena is sought is to obtain the identity of an alleged infringer and that such information will only be used for the purpose of protecting rights under this title.

(3) Contents of subpoena. The subpoena shall authorize and order the service provider receiving the notification and the subpoena to expeditiously disclose to the copyright owner or person authorized by the copyright owner information sufficient to identify the alleged infringer of the material described in the notification to the extent such information is available to the service provider.

(4) Basis for granting subpoena. If the notification filed satisfies the provisions of subsection (C)(3)(A), the proposed subpoena is in proper form, and the accompanying declaration is properly executed, the clerk shall expeditiously issue and sign the proposed subpoena and return it to the requester for delivery to the service provider.

(5) Actions of service provider receiving subpoena. Upon receipt of the issued subpoena, either accompanying or subsequent to the receipt of a notification described in subsection (C)(3)(A), the service provider shall expeditiously disclose to the copyright owner or person authorized by the copyright owner the information required by the subpoena, notwithstanding any other provision of law and regardless of whether the service provider responds to the notification.

(6) Rules applicable to subpoena. Unless otherwise provided by this section or by applicable rules of the court, the procedure for issuance and delivery of the subpoena, and the remedies for noncompliance with the subpoena, shall be governed to the greatest extent practicable by those provisions of the Federal Rules of Civil Procedure governing the issuance, service, and enforcement of a subpoena duces tecum.

(i) Conditions for eligibility.

(1) Accommodation of technology. The limitations on liability established by this section shall apply to a service provider only if the service provider

(A) has adopted and reasonably implemented, and informs subscribers and account holders of the service provider's system or network of, a policy that provides for the termination in appropriate circumstances of subscribers and account holders of the service provider's system or network who are repeat infringers; and

(B) accommodates and does not interfere with standard technical measures.

(2) Definition. As used in this subsection, the term "standard technical measures" means technical measures that are used by copyright owners to identify or protect copyrighted works and

(A) have been developed pursuant to a broad consensus of copyright owners and service providers in an open, fair, voluntary, multi-industry standards process;

(B) are available to any person on reasonable and nondiscriminatory terms; and

(C) do not impose substantial costs on service providers or substantial burdens on their systems or networks.

(j) Injunctions. The following rules shall apply in the case of any application for an injunction under section 502 against a service provider that is not subject to monetary remedies under this section:

(1) Scope of relief.

(A) With respect to conduct other than that which qualifies for the limitation on remedies set forth in subsection (a), the court may grant injunctive relief with respect to a service provider only in one or more of the following forms:

(i) An order restraining the service provider from providing access to infringing material or activity residing at a particular online site on the provider's system or network.

(ii) An order restraining the service provider from providing access to a subscriber or account holder of the service provider's system or network who is engaging in infringing activity and is identified in the order, by terminating the accounts of the subscriber or account holder that are specified in the order.

(iii) Such other injunctive relief as the court may consider necessary to prevent or restrain infringement of copyrighted material specified in the order of the court at a particular online location, if such relief is the least burdensome to the service provider among the forms of relief comparably effective for that purpose.

(B) If the service provider qualifies for the limitation on remedies described in subsection (a), the court may only grant injunctive relief in one or both of the following forms:

(i) An order restraining the service provider from providing access to a subscriber or account holder of the service provider's system or network who is using the provider's service to engage in infringing activity and is identified in the order, by terminating the accounts of the subscriber or account holder that are specified in the order.

(ii) An order restraining the service provider from providing access, by taking reasonable steps specified in the order to block access, to a specific, identified, online location outside the United States.

(2) Considerations. The court, in considering the relevant criteria for injunctive relief under applicable law, shall consider

> (A) whether such an injunction, either alone or in combination with other such injunctions issued against the same service provider under this subsection, would significantly burden either the provider or the operation of the provider's system or network;

> (B) the magnitude of the harm likely to be suffered by the copyright owner in the digital network environment if steps are not taken to prevent or restrain the infringement;

> (C) whether implementation of such an injunction would be technically feasible and effective, and would not interfere with access to noninfringing material at other online locations; and

> (D) whether other less burdensome and comparably effective means of preventing or restraining access to the infringing material are available.

(3) Notice and ex parte orders. Injunctive relief under this subsection shall be available only after notice to the service provider and an opportunity for the service provider to appear are provided, except for orders ensuring the preservation of evidence or other orders having no material adverse effect on the operation of the service provider's communications network.

(k) Definitions.

> (1) Service provider.

>> (A) As used in subsection (a), the term "service provider" means an entity offering the transmission, routing, or providing of connections for digital online communications, between or among points specified by a user, of material of the user's choosing, without modification to the content of the material as sent or received.

>> (B) As used in this section, other than subsection (a), the term "service provider" means a provider of online services or network access, or the operator of facilities therefor, and includes an entity described in subparagraph (A).

> (2) Monetary relief. As used in this section, the term "monetary relief" means damages, costs, attorneys' fees, and any other form of monetary payment.

(l) Other defenses not affected. The failure of a service provider's conduct to qualify for limitation of liability under this section shall not bear adversely upon the consideration of a defense by the service provider that the service provider's conduct is not infringing under this title or any other defense.

(m) Protection of privacy. Nothing in this section shall be construed to condition the applicability of subsections (a) through (d) on

> (1) a service provider monitoring its service or affirmatively seeking facts indicating infringing activity, except to the extent consistent with a standard technical measure complying with the provisions of subsection (i); or

> (2) a service provider gaining access to, removing, or disabling access to material in cases in which such conduct is prohibited by law.

# Intermediary Liability for Civil Offenses

# SECTION 230 OF THE COMMUNICATIONS ACT OF 1934 (1996)

*47 USC § 230 (passed as part of the Communications Decency Act of 1996, and as amended over time, including in 2017 by the Allow States and Victims to Fight Online Sex Trafficking Act, commonly known as "FOSTA")*

Protection for Private Blocking and Screening of Offensive Materials:

(a) Findings. The Congress finds the following:

(1) The rapidly developing array of Internet and other interactive computer services available to individual Americans represent an extraordinary advance in the availability of educational and informational resources to our citizens.

(2) These services offer users a great degree of control over the information that they receive, as well as the potential for even greater control in the future as technology develops.

(3) The Internet and other interactive computer services offer a forum for a true diversity of political discourse, unique opportunities for cultural development, and myriad avenues for intellectual activity.

(4) The Internet and other interactive computer services have flourished, to the benefit of all Americans, with a minimum of government regulation.

(5) Increasingly Americans are relying on interactive media for a variety of political, educational, cultural, and entertainment services.

(b) Policy. It is the policy of the United States--

(1) to promote the continued development of the Internet and other interactive computer services and other interactive media;

(2) to preserve the vibrant and competitive free market that presently exists for the Internet and other interactive computer services, unfettered by Federal or State regulation;

(3) to encourage the development of technologies which maximize user control over what information is received by individuals, families, and schools who use the Internet and other interactive computer services;

(4) to remove disincentives for the development and utilization of blocking and filtering technologies that empower parents to restrict their children's access to objectionable or inappropriate online material; and

(5) to ensure vigorous enforcement of Federal criminal laws to deter and punish trafficking in obscenity, stalking, and harassment by means of computer.

(c) Protection for "Good Samaritan" blocking and screening of offensive material

(1) Treatment of publisher or speaker

No provider or user of an interactive computer service shall be treated as the publisher or speaker of any information provided by another information content provider.

(2) Civil liability

No provider or user of an interactive computer service shall be held liable on account of--

> (A) any action voluntarily taken in good faith to restrict access to or availability of material that the provider or user considers to be obscene, lewd, lascivious, filthy, excessively violent, harassing, or otherwise objectionable, whether or not such material is constitutionally protected; or

> (B) any action taken to enable or make available to information content providers or others the technical means to restrict access to material described in paragraph (1).[1]

(d) Obligations of interactive computer service

A provider of interactive computer service shall, at the time of entering an agreement with a customer for the provision of interactive computer service and in a manner deemed appropriate by the provider, notify such customer that parental control protections (such as computer hardware, software, or filtering services) are commercially available that may assist the customer in limiting access to material that is harmful to minors. Such notice shall identify, or provide the customer with access to information identifying, current providers of such protections.

(e) Effect on other laws

> (1) No effect on criminal law

Nothing in this section shall be construed to impair the enforcement of section 223 or 231 of this title, chapter 71 (relating to obscenity) or 110 (relating to sexual exploitation of children) of Title 18, or any other Federal criminal statute.

(2) No effect on intellectual property law

Nothing in this section shall be construed to limit or expand any law pertaining to intellectual property.

(3) State law

Nothing in this section shall be construed to prevent any State from enforcing any State law that is consistent with this section. No cause of action may be brought and no liability may be imposed under any State or local law that is inconsistent with this section.

(4) No effect on communications privacy law

Nothing in this section shall be construed to limit the application of the Electronic Communications Privacy Act of 1986 or any of the amendments made by such Act, or any similar State law.

(5) No effect on sex trafficking law

Nothing in this section (other than subsection (c)(2)(A)) shall be construed to impair or limit--

> (A) any claim in a civil action brought under section 1595 of Title 18, if the conduct underlying the claim constitutes a violation of section 1591 of that title;

> (B) any charge in a criminal prosecution brought under State law if the conduct underlying the charge would constitute a violation of section 1591 of Title 18; or

(C) any charge in a criminal prosecution brought under State law if the conduct underlying the charge would constitute a violation of section 2421A of Title 18, and promotion or facilitation of prostitution is illegal in the jurisdiction where the defendant's promotion or facilitation of prostitution was targeted.

(f) Definitions

As used in this section:

(1) Internet

The term "Internet" means the international computer network of both Federal and non-Federal interoperable packet switched data networks.

(2) Interactive computer service

The term "interactive computer service" means any information service, system, or access software provider that provides or enables computer access by multiple users to a computer server, including specifically a service or system that provides access to the Internet and such systems operated or services offered by libraries or educational institutions.

(3) Information content provider

The term "information content provider" means any person or entity that is responsible, in whole or in part, for the creation or development of information provided through the Internet or any other interactive computer service.

(4) Access software provider

The term "access software provider" means a provider of software (including client or server software), or enabling tools that do any one or more of the following:

(A) filter, screen, allow, or disallow content;

(B) pick, choose, analyze, or digest content; or

(C) transmit, receive, display, forward, cache, search, subset, organize, reorganize, or translate content.

# Privacy and Data Protection

# COMPUTER FRAUD AND ABUSE ACT (CFAA)
## *18 U.S.C. §1030*

(a) Whoever—

(1) having knowingly accessed a computer without authorization or exceeding authorized access, and by means of such conduct having obtained information that has been determined by the United States Government pursuant to an Executive order or statute to require protection against unauthorized disclosure for reasons of national defense or foreign relations, or any restricted data, as defined in paragraph y. of section 11 of the Atomic Energy Act of 1954, with reason to believe that such information so obtained could be used to the injury of the United States, or to the advantage of any foreign nation willfully communicates, delivers, transmits, or causes to be communicated, delivered, or transmitted, or attempts to communicate, deliver, transmit or cause to be communicated, delivered, or transmitted the same to any person not entitled to receive it, or willfully retains the same and fails to deliver it to the officer or employee of the United States entitled to receive it;

(2) intentionally accesses a computer without authorization or exceeds authorized access, and thereby obtains—

> (A) information contained in a financial record of a financial institution, or of a card issuer as defined in section 1602(n) [1] of title 15, or contained in a file of a consumer reporting agency on a consumer, as such terms are defined in the Fair Credit Reporting Act (15 U.S.C. 1681 et seq.);

> (B) information from any department or agency of the United States; or

> (C) information from any protected computer;

(3) intentionally, without authorization to access any nonpublic computer of a department or agency of the United States, accesses such a computer of that department or agency that is exclusively for the use of the Government of the United States or, in the case of a computer not exclusively for such use, is used by or for the Government of the United States and such conduct affects that use by or for the Government of the United States;

(4) knowingly and with intent to defraud, accesses a protected computer without authorization, or exceeds authorized access, and by means of such conduct furthers the intended fraud and obtains anything of value, unless the object of the fraud and the thing obtained consists only of the use of the computer and the value of such use is not more than $5,000 in any 1-year period;

(5)

> (A) knowingly causes the transmission of a program, information, code, or command, and as a result of such conduct, intentionally causes damage without authorization, to a protected computer;

> (B) intentionally accesses a protected computer without authorization, and as a result of such conduct, recklessly causes damage; or

(C) intentionally accesses a protected computer without authorization, and as a result of such conduct, causes damage and loss.[2]

(6) knowingly and with intent to defraud traffics (as defined in section 1029) in any password or similar information through which a computer may be accessed without authorization, if—

(A) such trafficking affects interstate or foreign commerce; or

(B) such computer is used by or for the Government of the United States; [3]

(7) with intent to extort from any person any money or other thing of value, transmits in interstate or foreign commerce any communication containing any—

(A) threat to cause damage to a protected computer;

(B) threat to obtain information from a protected computer without authorization or in excess of authorization or to impair the confidentiality of information obtained from a protected computer without authorization or by exceeding authorized access; or

(C) demand or request for money or other thing of value in relation to damage to a protected computer, where such damage was caused to facilitate the extortion;

shall be punished as provided in subsection (c) of this section.

(b) Whoever conspires to commit or attempts to commit an offense under subsection (a) of this section shall be punished as provided in subsection (c) of this section.

(c) The punishment for an offense under subsection (a) or (b) of this section is—

(1)    (A) a fine under this title or imprisonment for not more than ten years, or both, in the case of an offense under subsection (a)(1) of this section which does not occur after a conviction for another offense under this section, or an attempt to commit an offense punishable under this subparagraph; and

(B) a fine under this title or imprisonment for not more than twenty years, or both, in the case of an offense under subsection (a)(1) of this section which occurs after a conviction for another offense under this section, or an attempt to commit an offense punishable under this subparagraph;

(2)    (A) except as provided in subparagraph (B), a fine under this title or imprisonment for not more than one year, or both, in the case of an offense under subsection (a)(2), (a)(3), or (a)(6) of this section which does not occur after a conviction for another offense under this section, or an attempt to commit an offense punishable under this subparagraph;

(B) a fine under this title or imprisonment for not more than 5 years, or both, in the case of an offense under subsection (a)(2), or an attempt to commit an offense punishable under this subparagraph, if—

(i) the offense was committed for purposes of commercial advantage or private financial gain;

(ii) the offense was committed in furtherance of any criminal or tortious act in violation of the Constitution or laws of the United States or of any State; or

(iii) the value of the information obtained exceeds $5,000; and

(C) a fine under this title or imprisonment for not more than ten years, or both, in the case of an offense under subsection (a)(2), (a)(3) or (a)(6) of this section which occurs after a conviction for another offense under this section, or an attempt to commit an offense punishable under this subparagraph;

(3)     (A) a fine under this title or imprisonment for not more than five years, or both, in the case of an offense under subsection (a)(4) or (a)(7) of this section which does not occur after a conviction for another offense under this section, or an attempt to commit an offense punishable under this subparagraph; and

(B) a fine under this title or imprisonment for not more than ten years, or both, in the case of an offense under subsection (a)(4),[4] or (a)(7) of this section which occurs after a conviction for another offense under this section, or an attempt to commit an offense punishable under this subparagraph;

(4)     (A) except as provided in subparagraphs (E) and (F), a fine under this title, imprisonment for not more than 5 years, or both, in the case of—

(i) an offense under subsection (a)(5)(B), which does not occur after a conviction for another offense under this section, if the offense caused (or, in the case of an attempted offense, would, if completed, have caused)—

(I) loss to 1 or more persons during any 1-year period (and, for purposes of an investigation, prosecution, or other proceeding brought by the United States only, loss resulting from a related course of conduct affecting 1 or more other protected computers) aggregating at least $5,000 in value;

(II) the modification or impairment, or potential modification or impairment, of the medical examination, diagnosis, treatment, or care of 1 or more individuals;

(III) physical injury to any person;

(IV) a threat to public health or safety;

(V) damage affecting a computer used by or for an entity of the United States Government in furtherance of the administration of justice, national defense, or national security; or

(VI) damage affecting 10 or more protected computers during any 1-year period; or

(ii) an attempt to commit an offense punishable under this subparagraph;

(B) except as provided in subparagraphs (E) and (F), a fine under this title, imprisonment for not more than 10 years, or both, in the case of—

(i) an offense under subsection (a)(5)(A), which does not occur after a conviction for another offense under this section, if the offense caused (or, in the case of an attempted offense, would, if completed, have caused) a harm provided in subclauses (I) through (VI) of subparagraph (A)(i); or

(ii) an attempt to commit an offense punishable under this subparagraph;

(C) except as provided in subparagraphs (E) and (F), a fine under this title, imprisonment for not more than 20 years, or both, in the case of—

(i) an offense or an attempt to commit an offense under subparagraphs (A) or (B) of subsection (a)(5) that occurs after a conviction for another offense under this section; or

(ii) an attempt to commit an offense punishable under this subparagraph;

(D) a fine under this title, imprisonment for not more than 10 years, or both, in the case of—

(i) an offense or an attempt to commit an offense under subsection (a)(5)(C) that occurs after a conviction for another offense under this section; or

(ii) an attempt to commit an offense punishable under this subparagraph;

(E) if the offender attempts to cause or knowingly or recklessly causes serious bodily injury from conduct in violation of subsection (a)(5)(A), a fine under this title, imprisonment for not more than 20 years, or both;

(F) if the offender attempts to cause or knowingly or recklessly causes death from conduct in violation of subsection (a)(5)(A), a fine under this title, imprisonment for any term of years or for life, or both; or

(G) a fine under this title, imprisonment for not more than 1 year, or both, for—

(i) any other offense under subsection (a)(5); or

(ii) an attempt to commit an offense punishable under this subparagraph.

(d)      (1) The United States Secret Service shall, in addition to any other agency having such authority, have the authority to investigate offenses under this section.

(2) The Federal Bureau of Investigation shall have primary authority to investigate offenses under subsection (a)(1) for any cases involving espionage, foreign counterintelligence, information protected

against unauthorized disclosure for reasons of national defense or foreign relations, or Restricted Data (as that term is defined in section 11y of the Atomic Energy Act of 1954 (42 U.S.C. 2014(y)), except for offenses affecting the duties of the United States Secret Service pursuant to section 3056(a) of this title.

(3) Such authority shall be exercised in accordance with an agreement which shall be entered into by the Secretary of the Treasury and the Attorney General.

(e) As used in this section—

(1) the term "computer" means an electronic, magnetic, optical, electrochemical, or other high speed data processing device performing logical, arithmetic, or storage functions, and includes any data storage facility or communications facility directly related to or operating in conjunction with such device, but such term does not include an automated typewriter or typesetter, a portable hand held calculator, or other similar device;

(2) the term "protected computer" means a computer—

(A) exclusively for the use of a financial institution or the United States Government, or, in the case of a computer not exclusively for such use, used by or for a financial institution or the United States Government and the conduct constituting the offense affects that use by or for the financial institution or the Government; or

(B) which is used in or affecting interstate or foreign commerce or communication, including a computer located outside the United States that is used in a manner that affects interstate or foreign commerce or communication of the United States;

(3) the term "State" includes the District of Columbia, the Commonwealth of Puerto Rico, and any other commonwealth, possession or territory of the United States;

(4) the term "financial institution" means—

(A) an institution, with deposits insured by the Federal Deposit Insurance Corporation;

(B) the Federal Reserve or a member of the Federal Reserve including any Federal Reserve Bank;

(C) a credit union with accounts insured by the National Credit Union Administration;

(D) a member of the Federal home loan bank system and any home loan bank;

(E) any institution of the Farm Credit System under the Farm Credit Act of 1971;

(F) a broker-dealer registered with the Securities and Exchange Commission pursuant to section 15 of the Securities Exchange Act of 1934;

(G) the Securities Investor Protection Corporation;

(H) a branch or agency of a foreign bank (as such terms are defined in paragraphs (1) and (3) of section 1(b) of the International Banking Act of 1978); and

        (I) an organization operating under section 25 or section 25(a) 1 of the Federal Reserve Act;

(5) the term "financial record" means information derived from any record held by a financial institution pertaining to a customer's relationship with the financial institution;

(6) the term "exceeds authorized access" means to access a computer with authorization and to use such access to obtain or alter information in the computer that the accesser is not entitled so to obtain or alter;

(7) the term "department of the United States" means the legislative or judicial branch of the Government or one of the executive departments enumerated in section 101 of title 5;

(8) the term "damage" means any impairment to the integrity or availability of data, a program, a system, or information;

(9) the term "government entity" includes the Government of the United States, any State or political subdivision of the United States, any foreign country, and any state, province, municipality, or other political subdivision of a foreign country;

(10) the term "conviction" shall include a conviction under the law of any State for a crime punishable by imprisonment for more than 1 year, an element of which is unauthorized access, or exceeding authorized access, to a computer;

(11) the term "loss" means any reasonable cost to any victim, including the cost of responding to an offense, conducting a damage assessment, and restoring the data, program, system, or information to its condition prior to the offense, and any revenue lost, cost incurred, or other consequential damages incurred because of interruption of service; and

(12) the term "person" means any individual, firm, corporation, educational institution, financial institution, governmental entity, or legal or other entity.

(f) This section does not prohibit any lawfully authorized investigative, protective, or intelligence activity of a law enforcement agency of the United States, a State, or a political subdivision of a State, or of an intelligence agency of the United States.

(g) Any person who suffers damage or loss by reason of a violation of this section may maintain a civil action against the violator to obtain compensatory damages and injunctive relief or other equitable relief. A civil action for a violation of this section may be brought only if the conduct involves 1 of the factors set forth in subclauses [5] (I), (II), (III), (IV), or (V) of subsection (c)(4)(A)(i). Damages for a violation involving only conduct described in subsection (c)(4)(A)(i)(I) are limited to economic damages. No action may be brought under this subsection unless such action is begun within 2 years of the date of the act complained of or the date of the discovery of the damage. No action may be brought under this subsection for the negligent design or manufacture of computer hardware, computer software, or firmware.

(h) The Attorney General and the Secretary of the Treasury shall report to the Congress annually, during the first 3 years following the date of the enactment of this subsection, concerning investigations and prosecutions under subsection (a)(5).

(i)       (1) The court, in imposing sentence on any person convicted of a violation of this section, or convicted of conspiracy to violate this section, shall order, in addition to any other sentence imposed and irrespective of any provision of State law, that such person forfeit to the United States—

> (A) such person's interest in any personal property that was used or intended to be used to commit or to facilitate the commission of such violation; and

> (B) any property, real or personal, constituting or derived from, any proceeds that such person obtained, directly or indirectly, as a result of such violation.

(2) The criminal forfeiture of property under this subsection, any seizure and disposition thereof, and any judicial proceeding in relation thereto, shall be governed by the provisions of section 413 of the Comprehensive Drug Abuse Prevention and Control Act of 1970 (21 U.S.C. 853), except subsection (d) of that section.

(j) For purposes of subsection (i), the following shall be subject to forfeiture to the United States and no property right shall exist in them:

(1) Any personal property used or intended to be used to commit or to facilitate the commission of any violation of this section, or a conspiracy to violate this section.

(2) Any property, real or personal, which constitutes or is derived from proceeds traceable to any violation of this section, or a conspiracy to violate this section

# FEDERAL TRADE COMMISSION ACT, SECTION 5

## 15 U.S.C.A. § 45

### (a) Declaration of unlawfulness; power to prohibit unfair practices; inapplicability to foreign trade

**(1)** Unfair methods of competition in or affecting commerce, and unfair or deceptive acts or practices in or affecting commerce, are hereby declared unlawful.

**(2)** The Commission is hereby empowered and directed to prevent persons, partnerships, or corporations, except banks, savings and loan institutions described in section 57a(f)(3) of this title, Federal credit unions described in section 57a(f)(4) of this title, common carriers subject to the Acts to regulate commerce, air carriers and foreign air carriers subject to part A of subtitle VII of Title 49, and persons, partnerships, or corporations insofar as they are subject to the Packers and Stockyards Act, 1921, as amended, except as provided in section 406(b) of said Act, from using unfair methods of competition in or affecting commerce and unfair or deceptive acts or practices in or affecting commerce.

**(3)** This subsection shall not apply to unfair methods of competition involving commerce with foreign nations (other than import commerce) unless—

**(A)** such methods of competition have a direct, substantial, and reasonably foreseeable effect--

**(i)** on commerce which is not commerce with foreign nations, or on import commerce with foreign nations; or

**(ii)** on export commerce with foreign nations, of a person engaged in such commerce in the United States; and

**(B)** such effect gives rise to a claim under the provisions of this subsection, other than this paragraph.

If this subsection applies to such methods of competition only because of the operation of subparagraph (A)(ii), this subsection shall apply to such conduct only for injury to export business in the United States.

**(4)** **(A)** For purposes of subsection (a), the term "unfair or deceptive acts or practices" includes such acts or practices involving foreign commerce that--

**(i)** cause or are likely to cause reasonably foreseeable injury within the United States; or

**(ii)** involve material conduct occurring within the United States.

**(B)** All remedies available to the Commission with respect to unfair and deceptive acts or practices shall be available for acts and practices described in this paragraph, including restitution to domestic or foreign victims. ***

### (l) Penalty for violation of order; injunctions and other appropriate equitable relief

Any person, partnership, or corporation who violates an order of the Commission after it has become final, and while such order is in effect, shall forfeit and pay to the United States a civil penalty of not more than $10,000 for each violation, which shall accrue to the United States and may be recovered in a civil action brought by the Attorney General of the United States. Each separate violation of such an order shall be a separate offense, except that in a case of a violation through continuing failure to obey or neglect to obey a final order of the Commission, each day of continuance of such failure or neglect shall be deemed a separate offense. In such actions, the United States district courts are empowered to grant mandatory injunctions and such other and further equitable relief as they deem appropriate in the enforcement of such final orders of the Commission. ***

### (n) Standard of proof; public policy considerations

The Commission shall have no authority under this section or section 57a of this title to declare unlawful an act or practice on the grounds that such act or practice is unfair unless the act or practice causes or is likely to cause substantial injury to consumers which is not reasonably avoidable by consumers themselves and not outweighed by countervailing benefits to consumers or to competition. In determining whether an act or practice is unfair, the Commission may consider established public policies as evidence to be considered with all other evidence. Such public policy considerations may not serve as a primary basis for such determination.

# ELECTRONIC COMMUNICATIONS PRIVACY ACT (ECPA) (1998): TITLE I (WIRETAP ACT)
## *18 U.S.C. §§ 2510-2511*

18 U.S. Code § 2510 - Definitions

As used in this chapter—

(1) "wire communication" means any aural transfer made in whole or in part through the use of facilities for the transmission of communications by the aid of wire, cable, or other like connection between the point of origin and the point of reception (including the use of such connection in a switching station) furnished or operated by any person engaged in providing or operating such facilities for the transmission of interstate or foreign communications or communications affecting interstate or foreign commerce;

(2) "oral communication" means any oral communication uttered by a person exhibiting an expectation that such communication is not subject to interception under circumstances justifying such expectation, but such term does not include any electronic communication;

(3) "State" means any State of the United States, the District of Columbia, the Commonwealth of Puerto Rico, and any territory or possession of the United States;

(4) "intercept" means the aural or other acquisition of the contents of any wire, electronic, or oral communication through the use of any electronic, mechanical, or other device.[1]

(5) "electronic, mechanical, or other device" means any device or apparatus which can be used to intercept a wire, oral, or electronic communication other than—

> (a) any telephone or telegraph instrument, equipment or facility, or any component thereof, (i) furnished to the subscriber or user by a provider of wire or electronic communication service in the ordinary course of its business and being used by the subscriber or user in the ordinary course of its business or furnished by such subscriber or user for connection to the facilities of such service and used in the ordinary course of its business; or (ii) being used by a provider of wire or electronic communication service in the ordinary course of its business, or by an investigative or law enforcement officer in the ordinary course of his duties;

> (b) a hearing aid or similar device being used to correct subnormal hearing to not better than normal;

(6) "person" means any employee, or agent of the United States or any State or political subdivision thereof, and any individual, partnership, association, joint stock company, trust, or corporation;

(7) "Investigative or law enforcement officer" means any officer of the United States or of a State or political subdivision thereof, who is empowered by law to conduct investigations of or to make arrests for offenses

enumerated in this chapter, and any attorney authorized by law to prosecute or participate in the prosecution of such offenses;

(8) "contents", when used with respect to any wire, oral, or electronic communication, includes any information concerning the substance, purport, or meaning of that communication;

(9) "Judge of competent jurisdiction" means—

(a) a judge of a United States district court or a United States court of appeals; and

(b) a judge of any court of general criminal jurisdiction of a State who is authorized by a statute of that State to enter orders authorizing interceptions of wire, oral, or electronic communications;

(10) "communication common carrier" has the meaning given that term in section 3 of the Communications Act of 1934;

(11) "aggrieved person" means a person who was a party to any intercepted wire, oral, or electronic communication or a person against whom the interception was directed;

(12) "electronic communication" means any transfer of signs, signals, writing, images, sounds, data, or intelligence of any nature transmitted in whole or in part by a wire, radio, electromagnetic, photoelectronic or photooptical system that affects interstate or foreign commerce, but does not include—

(A) any wire or oral communication;

(B) any communication made through a tone-only paging device;

(C) any communication from a tracking device (as defined in section 3117 of this title); or

(D) electronic funds transfer information stored by a financial institution in a communications system used for the electronic storage and transfer of funds;

(13) "user" means any person or entity who—

(A) uses an electronic communication service; and

(B) is duly authorized by the provider of such service to engage in such use;

(14) "electronic communications system" means any wire, radio, electromagnetic, photooptical or photoelectronic facilities for the transmission of wire or electronic communications, and any computer facilities or related electronic equipment for the electronic storage of such communications;

(15) "electronic communication service" means any service which provides to users thereof the ability to send or receive wire or electronic communications;

(16) "readily accessible to the general public" means, with respect to a radio communication, that such communication is not—

>    (A) scrambled or encrypted;

>    (B) transmitted using modulation techniques whose essential parameters have been withheld from the public with the intention of preserving the privacy of such communication;

>    (C) carried on a subcarrier or other signal subsidiary to a radio transmission;

>    (D) transmitted over a communication system provided by a common carrier, unless the communication is a tone only paging system communication; or

>    (E) transmitted on frequencies allocated under part 25, subpart D, E, or F of part 74, or part 94 of the Rules of the Federal Communications Commission, unless, in the case of a communication transmitted on a frequency allocated under part 74 that is not exclusively allocated to broadcast auxiliary services, the communication is a two-way voice communication by radio;

(17) "electronic storage" means—

>    (A) any temporary, intermediate storage of a wire or electronic communication incidental to the electronic transmission thereof; and

>    (B) any storage of such communication by an electronic communication service for purposes of backup protection of such communication;

(18) "aural transfer" means a transfer containing the human voice at any point between and including the point of origin and the point of reception;

(19) "foreign intelligence information", for purposes of section 2517(6) of this title, means—

>    (A) information, whether or not concerning a United Statesperson, that relates to the ability of the United States to protect against—

>>        (i) actual or potential attack or other grave hostile acts of a foreign power or an agent of a foreign power;

>>        (ii) sabotage or international terrorism by a foreign power or an agent of a foreign power; or

(iii) clandestine intelligence activities by an intelligence service or network of a foreign power or by an agent of a foreign power; or

(B) information, whether or not concerning a United Statesperson, with respect to a foreign power or foreign territory that relates to—

(i) the national defense or the security of the United States; or

(ii) the conduct of the foreign affairs of the United States;

(20) "protected computer" has the meaning set forth in section 1030; and

(21) "computer trespasser"—

(A) means a person who accesses a protected computer without authorization and thus has no reasonable expectation of privacy in any communication transmitted to, through, or from the protected computer; and

(B) does not include a person known by the owner or operator of the protected computer to have an existing contractual relationship with the owner or operator of the protected computer for access to all or part of the protected computer.

18 U.S. Code § 2511 – Interception and Disclosure of Wire, Oral, or Electronic Communications Prohibited

(1) Except as otherwise specifically provided in this chapter any person who—

(a) intentionally intercepts, endeavors to intercept, or procures any other person to intercept or endeavor to intercept, any wire, oral, or electronic communication;

(b) intentionally uses, endeavors to use, or procures any other person to use or endeavor to use any electronic, mechanical, or other device to intercept any oral communication when—

(i) such device is affixed to, or otherwise transmits a signal through, a wire, cable, or other like connection used in wire communication; or

(ii) such device transmits communications by radio, or interferes with the transmission of such communication; or

(iii) such person knows, or has reason to know, that such device or any component thereof has been sent through the mail or transported in interstate or foreign commerce; or

(iv) such use or endeavor to use (A) takes place on the premises of any business or other commercial establishment the operations of which affect interstate or foreign commerce; or

(B) obtains or is for the purpose of obtaining information relating to the operations of any business or other commercial establishment the operations of which affect interstate or foreign commerce; or

(v) such person acts in the District of Columbia, the Commonwealth of Puerto Rico, or any territory or possession of the United States;

(c) intentionally discloses, or endeavors to disclose, to any other person the contents of any wire, oral, or electronic communication, knowing or having reason to know that the information was obtained through the interception of a wire, oral, or electronic communication in violation of this subsection;

(d) intentionally uses, or endeavors to use, the contents of any wire, oral, or electronic communication, knowing or having reason to know that the information was obtained through the interception of a wire, oral, or electronic communication in violation of this subsection; or

(e) (i) intentionally discloses, or endeavors to disclose, to any other person the contents of any wire, oral, or electronic communication, intercepted by means authorized by sections 2511(2)(a)(ii), 2511(2)(b)–(c), 2511(2)(e), 2516, and 2518 of this chapter, (ii) knowing or having reason to know that the information was obtained through the interception of such a communication in connection with a criminal investigation, (iii) having obtained or received the information in connection with a criminal investigation, and (iv) with intent to improperly obstruct, impede, or interfere with a duly authorized criminal investigation,

shall be punished as provided in subsection (4) or shall be subject to suit as provided in subsection (5).

(2)

(a) (i) It shall not be unlawful under this chapter for an operator of a switchboard, or an officer, employee, or agent of a provider of wire or electronic communication service, whose facilities are used in the transmission of a wire or electronic communication, to intercept, disclose, or use that communication in the normal course of his employment while engaged in any activity which is a necessary incident to the rendition of his service or to the protection of the rights or property of the provider of that service, except that a provider of wire communication service to the public shall not utilize service observing or random monitoring except for mechanical or service quality control checks.

(ii) Notwithstanding any other law, providers of wire or electronic communication service, their officers, employees, and agents, landlords, custodians, or other persons, are authorized to provide information, facilities, or technical assistance to persons authorized by law to intercept wire, oral, or electronic communications or to conduct electronic surveillance, as defined in section 101 of the Foreign Intelligence Surveillance Act of 1978, if such provider, its officers, employees, or agents, landlord, custodian, or other specified person, has been provided with—

(A) a court order directing such assistance or a court order pursuant to section 704 of the Foreign Intelligence Surveillance Act of 1978 signed by the authorizing judge, or

(B) a certification in writing by a person specified in section 2518(7) of this title or the Attorney General of the United States that no warrant or court order is required by law, that all statutory requirements have been met, and that the specified assistance is required, setting forth the period of time during which the provision of the information, facilities, or technical assistance is authorized and specifying the information, facilities, or technical assistance required. No provider of wire or electronic communication service, officer, employee, or agent thereof, or landlord, custodian, or other specified person shall disclose the existence of any interception or surveillance or the device used to accomplish the interception or surveillance with respect to which the person has been furnished a court order or certification under this chapter, except as may otherwise be required by legal process and then only after prior notification to the Attorney General or to the principal prosecuting attorney of a State or any political subdivision of a State, as may be appropriate. Any such disclosure, shall render such person liable for the civil damages provided for in section 2520. No cause of action shall lie in any court against any provider of wire or electronic communication service, its officers, employees, or agents, landlord, custodian, or other specified person for providing information, facilities, or assistance in accordance with the terms of a court order, statutory authorization, or certification under this chapter.

(iii) If a certification under subparagraph (ii)(B) for assistance to obtain foreign intelligence information is based on statutory authority, the certification shall identify the specific statutory provision and shall certify that the statutory requirements have been met.

(b) It shall not be unlawful under this chapter for an officer, employee, or agent of the Federal Communications Commission, in the normal course of his employment and in discharge of the monitoring responsibilities exercised by the Commission in the enforcement of chapter 5 of title 47 of the United States Code, to intercept a wire or electronic communication, or oral communication transmitted by radio, or to disclose or use the information thereby obtained.

(c) It shall not be unlawful under this chapter for a person acting under color of law to intercept a wire, oral, or electronic communication, where such person is a party to the communication or one of the parties to the communication has given prior consent to such interception.

(d) It shall not be unlawful under this chapter for a person not acting under color of law to intercept a wire, oral, or electronic communication where such person is a party to the communication or where one of the parties to the communication has given prior consent to such interception unless such communication is intercepted for the purpose of committing any criminal or tortious act in violation of the Constitution or laws of the United States or of any State.

(e) Notwithstanding any other provision of this title or section 705 or 706 of the Communications Act of 1934, it shall not be unlawful for an officer, employee, or agent of the United States in the normal course of his official duty to conduct electronic surveillance, as defined in section 101 of the Foreign Intelligence Surveillance Act of 1978, as authorized by that Act.

(f) Nothing contained in this chapter or chapter 121 or 206 of this title, or section 705 of the Communications Act of 1934, shall be deemed to affect the acquisition by the United States Government of foreign intelligence information from international or foreign communications, or foreign intelligence activities conducted in accordance with otherwise applicable Federal law involving a foreign electronic communications system, utilizing a means other than electronic surveillance as defined in section 101 of the Foreign Intelligence Surveillance Act of 1978, and procedures in this chapter or chapter 121 and the Foreign Intelligence Surveillance Act of 1978 shall be the exclusive means by which electronic surveillance, as defined in section 101 of such Act, and the interception of domestic wire, oral, and electronic communications may be conducted.

(g) It shall not be unlawful under this chapter or chapter 121 of this title for any person—

> (i) to intercept or access an electronic communication made through an electronic communication system that is configured so that such electronic communication is readily accessible to the general public;
>
> (ii) to intercept any radio communication which is transmitted—
>
> > (I) by any station for the use of the general public, or that relates to ships, aircraft, vehicles, or persons in distress;
> >
> > (II) by any governmental, law enforcement, civil defense, private land mobile, or public safety communications system, including police and fire, readily accessible to the general public;
> >
> > (III) by a station operating on an authorized frequency within the bands allocated to the amateur, citizens band, or general mobile radio services; or
> >
> > (IV) by any marine or aeronautical communications system;
>
> (iii) to engage in any conduct which—
>
> > (I) is prohibited by section 633 of the Communications Act of 1934; or
> >
> > (II) is excepted from the application of section 705(a) of the Communications Act of 1934 by section 705(b) of that Act;

(iv) to intercept any wire or electronic communication the transmission of which is causing harmful interference to any lawfully operating station or consumer electronic equipment, to the extent necessary to identify the source of such interference; or

(v) for other users of the same frequency to intercept any radio communication made through a system that utilizes frequencies monitored by individuals engaged in the provision or the use of such system, if such communication is not scrambled or encrypted.

(h) It shall not be unlawful under this chapter—

(i) to use a pen register or a trap and trace device (as those terms are defined for the purposes of chapter 206 (relating to pen registers and trap and trace devices) of this title); or

(ii) for a provider of electronic communication service to record the fact that a wire or electronic communication was initiated or completed in order to protect such provider, another provider furnishing service toward the completion of the wire or electronic communication, or a user of that service, from fraudulent, unlawful or abusive use of such service.

(i) It shall not be unlawful under this chapter for a person acting under color of law to intercept the wire or electronic communications of a computer trespasser transmitted to, through, or from the protected computer, if—

(i) the owner or operator of the protected computer authorizes the interception of the computer trespasser's communications on the protected computer;

(ii) the person acting under color of law is lawfully engaged in an investigation;

(iii) the person acting under color of law has reasonable grounds to believe that the contents of the computer trespasser's communications will be relevant to the investigation; and

(iv) such interception does not acquire communications other than those transmitted to or from the computer trespasser.

(3)     (a) Except as provided in paragraph (b) of this subsection, a person or entity providing an electronic communication service to the public shall not intentionally divulge the contents of any communication (other than one to such person or entity, or an agent thereof) while in transmission on that service to any person or entity other than an addressee or intended recipient of such communication or an agent of such addressee or intended recipient.

(b) A person or entity providing electronic communication service to the public may divulge the contents of any such communication—

(i) as otherwise authorized in section 2511(2)(a) or 2517 of this title;

(ii) with the lawful consent of the originator or any addressee or intended recipient of such communication;

(iii) to a person employed or authorized, or whose facilities are used, to forward such communication to its destination; or

(iv) which were inadvertently obtained by the service provider and which appear to pertain to the commission of a crime, if such divulgence is made to a law enforcement agency.

(4)    (a) Except as provided in paragraph (b) of this subsection or in subsection (5), whoever violates subsection (1) of this section shall be fined under this title or imprisoned not more than five years, or both.

(b) Conduct otherwise an offense under this subsection that consists of or relates to the interception of a satellite transmission that is not encrypted or scrambled and that is transmitted—

(i) to a broadcasting station for purposes of retransmission to the general public; or

(ii) as an audio subcarrier intended for redistribution to facilities open to the public, but not including data transmissions or telephone calls, is not an offense under this subsection unless the conduct is for the purposes of direct or indirect commercial advantage or private financial gain.

(5)    (a)    (i) If the communication is—

(A) a private satellite video communication that is not scrambled or encrypted and the conduct in violation of this chapter is the private viewing of that communication and is not for a tortious or illegal purpose or for purposes of direct or indirect commercial advantage or private commercial gain; or

(B) a radio communication that is transmitted on frequencies allocated under subpart D of part 74 of the rules of the Federal Communications Commission that is not scrambled or encrypted and the conduct in violation of this chapter is not for a tortious or illegal purpose or for purposes of direct or indirect commercial advantage or private commercial gain, then the person who engages in such conduct shall be subject to suit by the Federal Government in a court of competent jurisdiction.

(ii) In an action under this subsection—

(A) if the violation of this chapter is a first offense for the person under paragraph (a) of subsection (4) and such person has not been found liable in a civil action under section 2520 of this title, the Federal Government shall be entitled to appropriate injunctive relief; and

(B) if the violation of this chapter is a second or subsequent offense under paragraph (a) of subsection (4) or such person has been found liable in any prior civil action under section 2520, the person shall be subject to a mandatory $500 civil fine.

(b) The court may use any means within its authority to enforce an injunction issued under paragraph (ii)(A), and shall impose a civil fine of not less than $500 for each violation of such an injunction.

# Stored Communications Act (1986)
## (Title II of Electronic Communications Privacy Act)
### *18 U.S.C. §§ 2701-2703*

**18 U.S. Code § 2701 – Unlawful Access to Stored Communications**

(a) Offense—Except as provided in subsection (c) of this section whoever—

(1) intentionally accesses without authorization a facility through which an electronic communication service is provided; or

(2) intentionally exceeds an authorization to access that facility; and thereby obtains, alters, or prevents authorized access to a wire or electronic communication while it is in electronic storage in such system shall be punished as provided in subsection (b) of this section.

(b)Punishment—The punishment for an offense under subsection (a) of this section is—

(1) if the offense is committed for purposes of commercial advantage, malicious destruction or damage, or private commercial gain, or in furtherance of any criminal or tortious act in violation of the Constitution or laws of the United States or any State—

(A) a fine under this title or imprisonment for not more than 5 years, or both, in the case of a first offense under this subparagraph; and

(B) a fine under this title or imprisonment for not more than 10 years, or both, for any subsequent offense under this subparagraph; and

(2) in any other case—

(A) a fine under this title or imprisonment for not more than 1 year or both, in the case of a first offense under this paragraph; and

(B) a fine under this title or imprisonment for not more than 5 years, or both, in the case of an offense under this subparagraph that occurs after a conviction of another offense under this section.

(c)Exceptions—Subsection (a) of this section does not apply with respect to conduct authorized—

(1) by the person or entity providing a wire or electronic communications service;

(2) by a user of that service with respect to a communication of or intended for that user; or

(3) in section 2703, 2704 or 2518 of this title.

## 18 U.S. Code § 2702 – Voluntary Disclosure of Customer Communications or Records

(a) Prohibitions. —Except as provided in subsection (b) or (c)—

(1) a person or entity providing an electronic communication service to the public shall not knowingly divulge to any person or entity the contents of a communication while in electronic storage by that service; and

(2) a person or entity providing remote computing service to the public shall not knowingly divulge to any person or entity the contents of any communication which is carried or maintained on that service—

(A) on behalf of, and received by means of electronic transmission from (or created by means of computer processing of communications received by means of electronic transmission from), a subscriber or customer of such service;

(B) solely for the purpose of providing storage or computer processing services to such subscriber or customer, if the provider is not authorized to access the contents of any such communications for purposes of providing any services other than storage or computer processing; and

(3) a provider of remote computing service or electronic communication service to the public shall not knowingly divulge a record or other information pertaining to a subscriber to or customer of such service (not including the contents of communications covered by paragraph (1) or (2)) to any governmental entity.

(b)Exceptions for disclosure of communications. —A provider described in subsection (a) may divulge the contents of a communication—

(1) to an addressee or intended recipient of such communication or an agent of such addressee or intended recipient;

(2) as otherwise authorized in section 2517, 2511(2)(a), or 2703 of this title;

(3) with the lawful consent of the originator or an addressee or intended recipient of such communication, or the subscriber in the case of remote computing service;

(4) to a person employed or authorized or whose facilities are used to forward such communication to its destination;

(5) as may be necessarily incident to the rendition of the service or to the protection of the rights or property of the provider of that service;

(6) to the National Center for Missing and Exploited Children, in connection with a report submitted thereto under section 2258A;

(7) to a law enforcement agency—

    (A) if the contents—

        (i) were inadvertently obtained by the service provider; and

        (ii) appear to pertain to the commission of a crime; or

    [(B) Repealed. Pub. L. 108–21, title V, § 508(b)(1)(A), Apr. 30, 2003, 117 Stat. 684]

(8) to a governmental entity, if the provider, in good faith, believes that an emergency involving danger of death or serious physical injury to any person requires disclosure without delay of communications relating to the emergency.

(c)Exceptions for Disclosure of Customer Records.—A provider described in subsection (a) may divulge a record or other information pertaining to a subscriber to or customer of such service (not including the contents of communications covered by subsection (a)(1) or (a)(2))—

(1) as otherwise authorized in section 2703;

(2) with the lawful consent of the customer or subscriber;

(3) as may be necessarily incident to the rendition of the service or to the protection of the rights or property of the provider of that service;

(4) to a governmental entity, if the provider, in good faith, believes that an emergency involving danger of death or serious physical injury to any person requires disclosure without delay of information relating to the emergency;

(5) to the National Center for Missing and Exploited Children, in connection with a report submitted thereto under section 2258A; or

(6) to any person other than a governmental entity.

(d)Reporting of Emergency Disclosures —On an annual basis, the Attorney General shall submit to the Committee on the Judiciary of the House of Representatives and the Committee on the Judiciary of the Senate a report containing—

(1) the number of accounts from which the Department of Justice has received voluntary disclosures under subsection (b)(8);

(2) a summary of the basis for disclosure in those instances where—

(A) voluntary disclosures under subsection (b)(8) were made to the Department of Justice; and

(B) the investigation pertaining to those disclosures was closed without the filing of criminal charges; and

(3) the number of accounts from which the Department of Justice has received voluntary disclosures under subsection (c)(4).

## 18 U.S. Code § 2703 – Required Disclosure of Customer Communications or Records

(a) Contents of Wire or Electronic Communications in Electronic Storage.— A governmental entity may require the disclosure by a provider of electronic communication service of the contents of a wire or electronic communication, that is in electronic storage in an electronic communications system for one hundred and eighty days or less, only pursuant to a warrant issued using the procedures described in the Federal Rules of Criminal Procedure (or, in the case of a State court, issued using State warrant procedures) by a court of competent jurisdiction. A governmental entity may require the disclosure by a provider of electronic communications services of the contents of a wire or electronic communication that has been in electronic storage in an electronic communications system for more than one hundred and eighty days by the means available under subsection (b) of this section.

(b) Contents of Wire or Electronic Communications in a Remote Computing Service. —

(1) A governmental entity may require a provider of remote computing service to disclose the contents of any wire or electronic communication to which this paragraph is made applicable by paragraph (2) of this subsection—

(A) without required notice to the subscriber or customer, if the governmental entity obtains a warrant issued using the procedures described in the Federal Rules of Criminal Procedure (or, in the case of a State court, issued using State warrant procedures) by a court of competent jurisdiction; or

(B) with prior notice from the governmental entity to the subscriber or customer if the governmental entity—

> > (i) uses an administrative subpoena authorized by a Federal or State statute or a Federal or State grand jury or trial subpoena; or
>
> > (ii) obtains a court order for such disclosure under subsection (d) of this section; except that delayed notice may be given pursuant to section 2705 of this title.

> (2) Paragraph (1) is applicable with respect to any wire or electronic communication that is held or maintained on that service—

> > (A) on behalf of, and received by means of electronic transmission from (or created by means of computer processing of communications received by means of electronic transmission from), a subscriber or customer of such remote computing service; and

> > (B) solely for the purpose of providing storage or computer processing services to such subscriber or customer, if the provider is not authorized to access the contents of any such communications for purposes of providing any services other than storage or computer processing.

(c)Records Concerning or Remote Computing Service. —

> (1) A governmental entity may require a provider of electronic communication service or remote computing service to disclose a record or other information pertaining to a subscriber to or customer of such service (not including the contents of communications) only when the governmental entity—

> > (A) obtains a warrant issued using the procedures described in the Federal Rules of Criminal Procedure (or, in the case of a State court, issued using State warrant procedures) by a court of competent jurisdiction;

> > (B) obtains a court order for such disclosure under subsection (d) of this section;

> > (C) has the consent of the subscriber or customer to such disclosure;

> > (D) submits a formal written request relevant to a law enforcement investigation concerning telemarketing fraud for the name, address, and place of business of a subscriber or customer of such provider, which subscriber or customer is engaged in telemarketing (as such term is defined in section 2325 of this title); or

> > (E) seeks information under paragraph (2).

> (2) A provider of electronic communication service or remote computing service shall disclose to a governmental entity the—

(A) name;

(B) address;

(C) local and long distance telephone connection records, or records of session times and durations;

(D) length of service (including start date) and types of service utilized;

(E) telephone or instrument number or other subscriber number or identity, including any temporarily assigned network address; and

(F) means and source of payment for such service (including any credit card or bank account number), of a subscriber to or customer of such service when the governmental entity uses an administrative subpoena authorized by a Federal or State statute or a Federal or State grand jury or trial subpoena or any means available under paragraph (1).

(3) A governmental entity receiving records or information under this subsection is not required to provide notice to a subscriber or customer.

(d) Requirements for Court Order. — A court order for disclosure under subsection (b) or (c) may be issued by any court that is a court of competent jurisdiction and shall issue only if the governmental entity offers specific and articulable facts showing that there are reasonable grounds to believe that the contents of a wire or electronic communication, or the records or other information sought, are relevant and material to an ongoing criminal investigation. In the case of a State governmental authority, such a court order shall not issue if prohibited by the law of such State. A court issuing an order pursuant to this section, on a motion made promptly by the service provider, may quash or modify such order, if the information or records requested are unusually voluminous in nature or compliance with such order otherwise would cause an undue burden on such provider.

(e)No Cause of Action Against a Provider Disclosing Information Under This Chapter. — No cause of action shall lie in any court against any provider of wire or electronic communication service, its officers, employees, agents, or other specified persons for providing information, facilities, or assistance in accordance with the terms of a court order, warrant, subpoena, statutory authorization, or certification under this chapter.

(f) Requirement to Preserve Evidence. —

(1) In general. — A provider of wire or electronic communication services or a remote computing service, upon the request of a governmental entity, shall take all necessary steps to preserve records and other evidence in its possession pending the issuance of a court order or other process.

(2) Period of retention. — Records referred to in paragraph (1) shall be retained for a period of 90 days, which shall be extended for an additional 90-day period upon a renewed request by the governmental entity.

(g)Presence of Officer Not Required. — Notwithstanding section 3105 of this title, the presence of an officer shall not be required for service or execution of a search warrant issued in accordance with this chapter requiring disclosure by a provider of electronic communications service or remote computing service of the contents of communications or records or other information pertaining to a subscriber to or customer of such service.

(h) Comity Analysis and Disclosure of Information Regarding Legal Process Seeking Contents of Wire or Electronic Communication. —

    (1) Definitions. —In this subsection—

        (A) the term "qualifying foreign government" means a foreign government—

            (i) with which the United States has an executive agreement that has entered into force under section 2523; and

            (ii) the laws of which provide to electronic communication service providers and remote computing service providers substantive and procedural opportunities similar to those provided under paragraphs (2) and (5); and

        (B) the term "United States person" has the meaning given the term in section 2523.

    (2) Motions to quash or modify. —

        (A) A provider of electronic communication service to the public or remote computing service, including a foreign electronic communication service or remote computing service, that is being required to disclose pursuant to legal process issued under this section the contents of a wire or electronic communication of a subscriber or customer, may file a motion to modify or quash the legal process where the provider reasonably believes—

            (i) that the customer or subscriber is not a United States person and does not reside in the United States; and

            (ii) that the required disclosure would create a material risk that the provider would violate the laws of a qualifying foreign government. Such a motion shall be filed not later than 14 days after the date on which the provider was served with the legal process, absent agreement with the government or permission from the court to extend the deadline based on an application made within the 14 days. The right to move to quash is without prejudice to any other grounds to move to quash or defenses thereto, but it shall be the sole basis for moving to quash on the grounds of a conflict of law related to a qualifying foreign government.

(B) Upon receipt of a motion filed pursuant to subparagraph (A), the court shall afford the governmental entity that applied for or issued the legal process under this section the opportunity to respond. The court may modify or quash the legal process, as appropriate, only if the court finds that—

(i) the required disclosure would cause the provider to violate the laws of a qualifying foreign government;

(ii) based on the totality of the circumstances, the interests of justice dictate that the legal process should be modified or quashed; and

(iii) the customer or subscriber is not a United States person and does not reside in the United States.

(3) Comity analysis. —For purposes of making a determination under paragraph (2)(B)(ii), the court shall take into account, as appropriate—

(A) the interests of the United States, including the investigative interests of the governmental entity seeking to require the disclosure;

(B) the interests of the qualifying foreign government in preventing any prohibited disclosure;

(C) the likelihood, extent, and nature of penalties to the provider or any employees of the provider as a result of inconsistent legal requirements imposed on the provider;

(D) the location and nationality of the subscriber or customer whose communications are being sought, if known, and the nature and extent of the subscriber or customer's connection to the United States, or if the legal process has been sought on behalf of a foreign authority pursuant to section 3512, the nature and extent of the subscriber or customer's connection to the foreign authority's country;

(E) the nature and extent of the provider's ties to and presence in the United States;

(F) the importance to the investigation of the information required to be disclosed;

(G) the likelihood of timely and effective access to the information required to be disclosed through means that would cause less serious negative consequences; and

(H) if the legal process has been sought on behalf of a foreign authority pursuant to section 3512, the investigative interests of the foreign authority making the request for assistance.

(4) Disclosure obligations during pendency of challenge. — A service provider shall preserve, but not be obligated to produce, information sought during the pendency of a motion brought under this subsection, unless the court finds that immediate production is necessary to prevent an adverse result identified in section 2705(a)(2).

(5) Disclosure to qualifying foreign government. —

(A) It shall not constitute a violation of a protective order issued under section 2705 for a provider of electronic communication service to the public or remote computing service to disclose to the entity within a qualifying foreign government, designated in an executive agreement under section 2523, the fact of the existence of legal process issued under this section seeking the contents of a wire or electronic communication of a customer or subscriber who is a national or resident of the qualifying foreign government.

(B) Nothing in this paragraph shall be construed to modify or otherwise affect any other authority to make a motion to modify or quash a protective order issued under section 2705.

# CONTROLLING THE ASSAULT OF NON-SOLICITED PORNOGRAPHY AND MARKETING ("CAN-SPAM") ACT (2003)

Article 1. Subject-matter and objectives

15 USCA § 7702

SEC. 3. DEFINITIONS.

In this Act:
(1) AFFIRMATIVE CONSENT.—The term "affirmative consent", when used with respect to a commercial electronic mail message, means that—
(A) the recipient expressly consented to receive the message, either in response to a clear and conspicuous request for such consent or at the recipient's own initiative; and
(B) if the message is from a party other than the party to which the recipient communicated such consent, the recipient was given clear and conspicuous notice at the time the consent was communicated that the recipient's electronic mail address could be transferred to such other party for the purpose of initiating commercial electronic mail messages.

(2) Commercial electronic mail message—
(A) IN GENERAL.—The term "commercial electronic mail message" means any electronic mail message the primary purpose of which is the commercial advertisement or promotion of a commercial product or service (including content on an Internet website operated for a commercial purpose).
(B) TRANSACTIONAL OR RELATIONSHIP MESSAGES.—The term "commercial electronic mail message" does not include a transactional or relationship message.
(C) REGULATIONS REGARDING PRIMARY PURPOSE.—Not later than 12 months after the date of the enactment of this Act, the Commission shall issue regulations pursuant to section 13 defining the relevant criteria to facilitate the determination of the primary purpose of an electronic mail message.
(D) REFERENCE TO COMPANY OR WEBSITE.—The inclusion of a reference to a commercial entity or a link to the website of a commercial entity in an electronic mail message does not, by itself, cause such message to be treated as a commercial electronic mail message for purposes of this Act if the contents or circumstances of the message indicate a primary purpose other than commercial advertisement or promotion of a commercial product or service.

(3) COMMISSION.—The term "Commission" means the Federal Trade Commission.

(4) DOMAIN NAME.—The term "domain name" means any alphanumeric designation which is registered with or assigned by any domain name registrar, domain name registry, or other domain name registration authority as part of an electronic address on the Internet.

(5) ELECTRONIC MAIL ADDRESS.—The term "electronic mail address" means a destination, commonly expressed as a string of characters, consisting of a unique user name or mailbox (commonly referred to as the "local part") and a reference to an Internet domain (commonly referred to as the "domain part"), whether or not displayed, to which an electronic mail message can be sent or delivered.

(6) ELECTRONIC MAIL MESSAGE.—The term "electronic mail message" means a message sent to a unique

electronic mail address.

(7) FTC ACT.—The term "FTC Act" means the Federal Trade Commission Act (15 U.S.C. 41 et seq.).

(8) HEADER INFORMATION.—The term "header information" means the source, destination, and routing information attached to an electronic mail message, including the originating domain name and originating electronic mail address, and any other information that appears in the line identifying, or purporting to identify, a person initiating the message.

(9) INITIATE.—The term "initiate", when used with respect to a commercial electronic mail message, means to originate or transmit such message or to procure the origination or transmission of such message, but shall not include actions that constitute routine conveyance of such message. For purposes of this paragraph, more than one person may be considered to have initiated a message.

(10) INTERNET.—The term "Internet" has the meaning given that term in the Internet Tax Freedom Act (47 U.S.C. 151 nt).

(11) INTERNET ACCESS SERVICE.—The term "Internet access service" has the meaning given that term in section 231(e)(4) of the Communications Act of 1934 (47 U.S.C. 231(e)(4)).

(12) PROCURE.—The term "procure", when used with respect to the initiation of a commercial electronic mail message, means intentionally to pay or provide other consideration to, or induce, another person to initiate such a message on one's behalf.

(13) PROTECTED COMPUTER.—The term "protected computer" has the meaning given that term in section 1030(e)(2)(B) of title 18, United States Code.

(14) RECIPIENT.—The term "recipient", when used with respect to a commercial electronic mail message, means an authorized user of the electronic mail address to which the message was sent or delivered. If a recipient of a commercial electronic mail message has one or more electronic mail addresses in addition to the address to which the message was sent or delivered, the recipient shall be treated as a separate recipient with respect to each such address. If an electronic mail address is reassigned to a new user, the new user shall not be treated as a recipient of any commercial electronic mail message sent or delivered to that address before it was reassigned.

(15) ROUTINE CONVEYANCE.—The term "routine conveyance" means the transmission, routing, relaying, handling, or storing, through an automatic technical process, of an electronic mail message for which another person has identified the recipients or provided the recipient addresses.

(16) SENDER.—
  (A) IN GENERAL.—Except as provided in subparagraph (B), the term "sender", when used with respect to a commercial electronic mail message, means a person who initiates such a message and whose product, service, or Internet web site is advertised or promoted by the message.
  (B) SEPARATE LINES OF BUSINESS OR DIVISIONS.—If an entity operates through separate lines of business or divisions and holds itself out to the recipient throughout the message as that particular line of business or division rather than as the entity of which such line of business or division is a part, then the line of business or the division shall be treated as the sender of such message for purposes of this Act.

(17) Transactional or relationship message—
  (A) IN GENERAL.—The term "transactional or relationship message" means an electronic mail message the

primary purpose of which is—

(i) to facilitate, complete, or confirm a commercial transaction that the recipient has previously agreed to enter into with the sender;

(ii) to provide warranty information, product recall information, or safety or security information with respect to a commercial product or service used or purchased by the recipient;

(iii) to provide—

(I) notification concerning a change in the terms or features of;

(II) notification of a change in the recipient's standing or status with respect to; or

(III) at regular periodic intervals, account balance information or other type of account statement with respect to, a subscription, membership, account, loan, or comparable ongoing commercial relationship involving the ongoing purchase or use by the recipient of products or services offered by the sender;

(iv) to provide information directly related to an employment relationship or related benefit plan in which the recipient is currently involved, participating, or enrolled; or

(v) to deliver goods or services, including product updates or upgrades, that the recipient is entitled to receive under the terms of a transaction that the recipient has previously agreed to enter into with the sender.

(B) MODIFICATION OF DEFINITION.—The Commission by regulation pursuant to section 13 may modify the definition in subparagraph (A) to expand or contract the categories of messages that are treated as transactional or relationship messages for purposes of this Act to the extent that such modification is necessary to accommodate changes in electronic mail technology or practices and accomplish the purposes of this Act.

18 USCA § 1037

§ 1037. Fraud and related activity in connection with electronic mail

(a) IN GENERAL.—Whoever, in or affecting interstate or foreign commerce, knowingly—

(1) accesses a protected computer without authorization, and intentionally initiates the transmission of multiple commercial electronic mail messages from or through such computer,

(2) uses a protected computer to relay or retransmit multiple commercial electronic mail messages, with the intent to deceive or mislead recipients, or any Internet access service, as to the origin of such messages,

(3) materially falsifies header information in multiple commercial electronic mail messages and intentionally initiates the transmission of such messages,

(4) registers, using information that materially falsifies the identity of the actual registrant, for five or more electronic mail accounts or online user accounts or two or more domain names, and intentionally initiates the transmission of multiple commercial electronic mail messages from any combination of such accounts or domain names, or

(5) falsely represents oneself to be the registrant or the legitimate successor in interest to the registrant of 5 or more Internet Protocol addresses, and intentionally initiates the transmission of multiple commercial electronic mail messages from such addresses, or conspires to do so, shall be punished as provided in subsection (b).

(b) PENALTIES.—The punishment for an offense under subsection (a) is—

(1) a fine under this title, imprisonment for not more than 5 years, or both, if—

(A) the offense is committed in furtherance of any felony under the laws of the United States or of any State; or

(B) the defendant has previously been convicted under this section or section 1030, or under the law of any State for conduct involving the transmission of multiple commercial electronic mail messages or unauthorized access to a computer system;

(2) a fine under this title, imprisonment for not more than 3 years, or both, if—

(A) the offense is an offense under subsection (a)(1);

(B) the offense is an offense under subsection (a)(4) and involved 20 or more falsified electronic mail or online user account registrations, or 10 or more falsified domain name registrations;

(C) the volume of electronic mail messages transmitted in furtherance of the offense exceeded 2,500 during any 24–hour period, 25,000 during any 30–day period, or 250,000 during any 1–year period;

(D) the offense caused loss to one or more persons aggregating $5,000 or more in value during any 1–year period;

(E) as a result of the offense any individual committing the offense obtained anything of value aggregating $5,000 or more during any 1–year period; or

(F) the offense was undertaken by the defendant in concert with three or more other persons with respect to whom the defendant occupied a position of organizer or leader; and

(3) a fine under this title or imprisonment for not more than 1 year, or both, in any other case.

(c) FORFEITURE.—

(1) IN GENERAL.—The court, in imposing sentence on a person who is convicted of an offense under this section, shall order that the defendant forfeit to the United States—

(A) any property, real or personal, constituting or traceable to gross proceeds obtained from such offense; and

(B) any equipment, software, or other technology used or intended to be used to commit or to facilitate the commission of such offense.

(2) PROCEDURES.—The procedures set forth in section 413 of the Controlled Substances Act (21 U.S.C. 853), other than subsection (d) of that section, and in Rule 32.2 of the Federal Rules of Criminal Procedure, shall apply to all stages of a criminal forfeiture proceeding under this section.

(d) DEFINITIONS.—In this section:

(1) LOSS.—The term 'loss' has the meaning given that term in section 1030(e) of this title.

(2) MATERIALLY.—For purposes of paragraphs (3) and (4) of subsection (a), header information or registration information is materially falsified if it is altered or concealed in a manner that would impair the ability of a recipient of the message, an Internet access service processing the message on behalf of a recipient, a person alleging a violation of this section, or a law enforcement agency to identify, locate, or respond to a person who initiated the electronic mail message or to investigate the alleged violation.

(3) MULTIPLE.—The term 'multiple' means more than 100 electronic mail messages during a 24–hour period, more than 1,000 electronic mail messages during a 30–day period, or more than 10,000 electronic mail messages during a 1–year period.

(4) OTHER TERMS.—Any other term has the meaning given that term by section 3 of the CAN–SPAM Act of 2003..

15 USCA § 7704

SEC. 5. OTHER PROTECTIONS FOR USERS OF COMMERCIAL ELECTRONIC MAIL.

(a) REQUIREMENTS FOR TRANSMISSION OF MESSAGES.—

(1) PROHIBITION OF FALSE OR MISLEADING TRANSMISSION INFORMATION.—It is unlawful for any person to initiate the transmission, to a protected computer, of a commercial electronic mail message, or a

transactional or relationship message, that contains, or is accompanied by, header information that is materially false or materially misleading. For purposes of this paragraph—

(A) header information that is technically accurate but includes an originating electronic mail address, domain name, or Internet Protocol address the access to which for purposes of initiating the message was obtained by means of false or fraudulent pretenses or representations shall be considered materially misleading;

(B) a "from" line (the line identifying or purporting to identify a person initiating the message) that accurately identifies any person who initiated the message shall not be considered materially false or materially misleading; and

(C) header information shall be considered materially misleading if it fails to identify accurately a protected computer used to initiate the message because the person initiating the message knowingly uses another protected computer to relay or retransmit the message for purposes of disguising its origin.

(2) PROHIBITION OF DECEPTIVE SUBJECT HEADINGS.—It is unlawful for any person to initiate the transmission to a protected computer of a commercial electronic mail message if such person has actual knowledge, or knowledge fairly implied on the basis of objective circumstances, that a subject heading of the message would be likely to mislead a recipient, acting reasonably under the circumstances, about a material fact regarding the contents or subject matter of the message (consistent with the criteria used in enforcement of section 5 of the Federal Trade Commission Act (15 U.S.C. 45)).

(3) Inclusion of return address or comparable mechanism in commercial electronic mail—

(A) IN GENERAL.—It is unlawful for any person to initiate the transmission to a protected computer of a commercial electronic mail message that does not contain a functioning return electronic mail address or other Internet-based mechanism, clearly and conspicuously displayed, that—

(i) a recipient may use to submit, in a manner specified in the message, a reply electronic mail message or other form of Internet-based communication requesting not to receive future commercial electronic mail messages from that sender at the electronic mail address where the message was received; and

(ii) remains capable of receiving such messages or communications for no less than 30 days after the transmission of the original message.

(B) MORE DETAILED OPTIONS POSSIBLE.—The person initiating a commercial electronic mail message may comply with subparagraph (A)(i) by providing the recipient a list or menu from which the recipient may choose the specific types of commercial electronic mail messages the recipient wants to receive or does not want to receive from the sender, if the list or menu includes an option under which the recipient may choose not to receive any commercial electronic mail messages from the sender.

(C) TEMPORARY INABILITY TO RECEIVE MESSAGES OR PROCESS REQUESTS.—A return electronic mail address or other mechanism does not fail to satisfy the requirements of subparagraph (A) if it is unexpectedly and temporarily unable to receive messages or process requests due to a technical problem beyond the control of the sender if the problem is corrected within a reasonable time period.

(4) PROHIBITION OF TRANSMISSION OF COMMERCIAL ELECTRONIC MAIL AFTER OBJECTION.—

(A) IN GENERAL.—If a recipient makes a request using a mechanism provided pursuant to paragraph (3) not to receive some or any commercial electronic mail messages from such sender, then it is unlawful—

(i) for the sender to initiate the transmission to the recipient, more than 10 business days after the receipt of such request, of a commercial electronic mail message that falls within the scope of the request;

(ii) for any person acting on behalf of the sender to initiate the transmission to the recipient, more than 10 business days after the receipt of such request, of a commercial electronic mail message with actual knowledge, or knowledge fairly implied on the basis of objective circumstances, that such message falls within the scope of the request;

(iii) for any person acting on behalf of the sender to assist in initiating the transmission to the recipient, through the provision or selection of addresses to which the message will be sent, of a commercial electronic mail message with actual knowledge, or knowledge fairly implied on the basis of objective circumstances, that such message would violate clause (i) or (ii); or

(iv) for the sender, or any other person who knows that the recipient has made such a request, to sell, lease, exchange, or otherwise transfer or release the electronic mail address of the recipient (including through any transaction or other transfer involving mailing lists bearing the electronic mail address of the recipient) for any purpose other than compliance with this Act or other provision of law.

(B) SUBSEQUENT AFFIRMATIVE CONSENT.—A prohibition in subparagraph (A) does not apply if there is affirmative consent by the recipient subsequent to the request under subparagraph (A).

(5) INCLUSION OF IDENTIFIER, OPT-OUT, AND PHYSICAL ADDRESS IN COMMERCIAL ELECTRONIC MAIL.—(A) It is unlawful for any person to initiate the transmission of any commercial electronic mail message to a protected computer unless the message provides—

(i) clear and conspicuous identification that the message is an advertisement or solicitation;

(ii) clear and conspicuous notice of the opportunity under paragraph (3) to decline to receive further commercial electronic mail messages from the sender; and

(iii) a valid physical postal address of the sender.

(B) Subparagraph (A)(i) does not apply to the transmission of a commercial electronic mail message if the recipient has given prior affirmative consent to receipt of the message.

(6) MATERIALLY.—For purposes of paragraph (1), the term "materially", when used with respect to false or misleading header information, includes the alteration or concealment of header information in a manner that would impair the ability of an Internet access service processing the message on behalf of a recipient, a person alleging a violation of this section, or a law enforcement agency to identify, locate, or respond to a person who initiated the electronic mail message or to investigate the alleged violation, or the ability of a recipient of the message to respond to a person who initiated the electronic message.

(b) Aggravated Violations Relating to Commercial Electronic Mail—

(1) Address harvesting and dictionary attacks—

(A) IN GENERAL.—It is unlawful for any person to initiate the transmission, to a protected computer, of a commercial electronic mail message that is unlawful under subsection (a), or to assist in the origination of such message through the provision or selection of addresses to which the message will be transmitted, if such person had actual knowledge, or knowledge fairly implied on the basis of objective circumstances, that—

(i) the electronic mail address of the recipient was obtained using an automated means from an Internet website or proprietary online service operated by another person, and such website or online service included, at the time the address was obtained, a notice stating that the operator of such website or online service will not give, sell, or otherwise transfer addresses maintained by such website or online service to any other party for the purposes of initiating, or enabling others to initiate, electronic mail messages; or

(ii) the electronic mail address of the recipient was obtained using an automated means that generates possible electronic mail addresses by combining names, letters, or numbers into numerous permutations.

(B) DISCLAIMER.—Nothing in this paragraph creates an ownership or proprietary interest in such electronic mail addresses.

(2) AUTOMATED CREATION OF MULTIPLE ELECTRONIC MAIL ACCOUNTS.—It is unlawful for any person to use scripts or other automated means to register for multiple electronic mail accounts or online user accounts from which to transmit to a protected computer, or enable another person to transmit to a protected computer, a commercial electronic mail message that is unlawful under subsection (a).

(3) RELAY OR RETRANSMISSION THROUGH UNAUTHORIZED ACCESS.—It is unlawful for any person knowingly to relay or retransmit a commercial electronic mail message that is unlawful under subsection (a) from a protected computer or computer network that such person has accessed without authorization.

(c) SUPPLEMENTARY RULEMAKING AUTHORITY.—The Commission shall by regulation, pursuant to section 13—

(1) modify the 10–business–day period under subsection (a)(4)(A) or subsection (a)(4)(B), or both, if the Commission determines that a different period would be more reasonable after taking into account—

(A) the purposes of subsection (a);

(B) the interests of recipients of commercial electronic mail; and

(C) the burdens imposed on senders of lawful commercial electronic mail; and

(2) specify additional activities or practices to which subsection (b) applies if the Commission determines that those activities or practices are contributing substantially to the proliferation of commercial electronic mail messages that are unlawful under subsection (a).

(d) REQUIREMENT TO PLACE WARNING LABELS ON COMMERCIAL ELECTRONIC MAIL CONTAINING SEXUALLY ORIENTED MATERIAL.—

(1) IN GENERAL.—No person may initiate in or affecting interstate commerce the transmission, to a protected computer, of any commercial electronic mail message that includes sexually oriented material and—

(A) fail to include in subject heading for the electronic mail message the marks or notices prescribed by the Commission under this subsection; or

(B) fail to provide that the matter in the message that is initially viewable to the recipient, when the message is opened by any recipient and absent any further actions by the recipient, includes only—

(i) to the extent required or authorized pursuant to paragraph (2), any such marks or notices;

(ii) the information required to be included in the message pursuant to subsection (a)(5); and

(iii) instructions on how to access, or a mechanism to access, the sexually oriented material.

(2) PRIOR AFFIRMATIVE CONSENT.—Paragraph (1) does not apply to the transmission of an electronic mail message if the recipient has given prior affirmative consent to receipt of the message.

(3) PRESCRIPTION OF MARKS AND NOTICES.—Not later than 120 days after the date of the enactment of this Act, the Commission in consultation with the Attorney General shall prescribe clearly identifiable marks or notices to be included in or associated with commercial electronic mail that contains sexually oriented material, in order to inform the recipient of that fact and to facilitate filtering of such electronic mail. The Commission shall publish in the Federal Register and provide notice to the public of the marks or notices prescribed under this paragraph.

(4) DEFINITION.—In this subsection, the term "sexually oriented material" means any material that depicts sexually explicit conduct (as that term is defined in section 2256 of title 18, United States Code), unless the depiction constitutes a small and insignificant part of the whole, the remainder of which is not primarily devoted to sexual matters.

(5) PENALTY.—Whoever knowingly violates paragraph (1) shall be fined under title 18, United States Code, or imprisoned not more than 5 years, or both.

15 USCA § 7705

## SEC. 6. BUSINESSES KNOWINGLY PROMOTED BY ELECTRONIC MAIL WITH FALSE OR MISLEADING TRANSMISSION INFORMATION.

(a) IN GENERAL.—It is unlawful for a person to promote, or allow the promotion of, that person's trade or business, or goods, products, property, or services sold, offered for sale, leased or offered for lease, or otherwise made available through that trade or business, in a commercial electronic mail message the transmission of which is in violation of section 5(a)(1) if that person—

(1) knows, or should have known in the ordinary course of that person's trade or business, that the goods, products, property, or services sold, offered for sale, leased or offered for lease, or otherwise made available through that trade or business were being promoted in such a message;

(2) received or expected to receive an economic benefit from such promotion; and

(3) took no reasonable action—

  (A) to prevent the transmission; or

  (B) to detect the transmission and report it to the Commission.

(b) Limited Enforcement Against Third Parties—

(1) IN GENERAL.—Except as provided in paragraph (2), a person (hereinafter referred to as the "third party") that provides goods, products, property, or services to another person that violates subsection (a) shall not be held liable for such violation.

(2) EXCEPTION.—Liability for a violation of subsection (a) shall be imputed to a third party that provides goods, products, property, or services to another person that violates subsection (a) if that third party—

  (A) owns, or has a greater than 50 percent ownership or economic interest in, the trade or business of the person that violated subsection (a); or

  (B)(i) has actual knowledge that goods, products, property, or services are promoted in a commercial electronic mail message the transmission of which is in violation of section 5(a)(1); and

  (ii) receives, or expects to receive, an economic benefit from such promotion.

(c) EXCLUSIVE ENFORCEMENT BY FTC.—Subsections (f) and (g) of section 7 do not apply to violations of this section.

(d) SAVINGS PROVISION.—Except as provided in section 7(f)(8), nothing in this section may be construed to limit or prevent any action that may be taken under this Act with respect to any violation of any other section of this Act.

<< 15 USCA § 7706 >>

SEC. 7. ENFORCEMENT GENERALLY.

(a) VIOLATION IS UNFAIR OR DECEPTIVE ACT OR PRACTICE.—Except as provided in subsection (b), this Act shall be enforced by the Commission as if the violation of this Act were an unfair or deceptive act or practice proscribed under section 18(a)(1)(B) of the Federal Trade Commission Act (15 U.S.C. 57a(a)(1)(B)).

(b) ENFORCEMENT BY CERTAIN OTHER AGENCIES.—Compliance with this Act shall be enforced—
  (1) under section 8 of the Federal Deposit Insurance Act (12 U.S.C. 1818), in the case of—
    (A) national banks, and Federal branches and Federal agencies of foreign banks, by the Office of the Comptroller of the Currency;
    (B) member banks of the Federal Reserve System (other than national banks), branches and agencies of foreign banks (other than Federal branches, Federal agencies, and insured State branches of foreign banks), commercial lending companies owned or controlled by foreign banks, organizations operating under section 25 or 25A of the Federal Reserve Act (12 U.S.C. 601 and 611), and bank holding companies, by the Board;
    (C) banks insured by the Federal Deposit Insurance Corporation (other than members of the Federal Reserve System) and insured State branches of foreign banks, by the Board of Directors of the Federal Deposit Insurance Corporation; and
    (D) savings associations the deposits of which are insured by the Federal Deposit Insurance Corporation, by the Director of the Office of Thrift Supervision;

(2) under the Federal Credit Union Act (12 U.S.C. 1751 et seq.) by the Board of the National Credit Union Administration with respect to any Federally insured credit union;

(3) under the Securities Exchange Act of 1934 (15 U.S.C. 78a et seq.) by the Securities and Exchange Commission with respect to any broker or dealer;

(4) under the Investment Company Act of 1940 (15 U.S.C. 80a–1 et seq.) by the Securities and Exchange Commission with respect to investment companies;

(5) under the Investment Advisers Act of 1940 (15 U.S.C. 80b–1 et seq.) by the Securities and Exchange Commission with respect to investment advisers registered under that Act;

(6) under State insurance law in the case of any person engaged in providing insurance, by the applicable State insurance authority of the State in which the person is domiciled, subject to section 104 of the Gramm–Bliley–Leach Act (15 U.S.C. 6701), except that in any State in which the State insurance authority elects not to exercise this power, the enforcement authority pursuant to this Act shall be exercised by the Commission in accordance with subsection (a);

(7) under part A of subtitle VII of title 49, United States Code, by the Secretary of Transportation with respect to any air carrier or foreign air carrier subject to that part;

(8) under the Packers and Stockyards Act, 1921 (7 U.S.C. 181 et seq.) (except as provided in section 406 of that Act (7 U.S.C. 226, 227)), by the Secretary of Agriculture with respect to any activities subject to that Act;

(9) under the Farm Credit Act of 1971 (12 U.S.C. 2001 et seq.) by the Farm Credit Administration with respect to any Federal land bank, Federal land bank association, Federal intermediate credit bank, or production credit association; and

(10) under the Communications Act of 1934 (47 U.S.C. 151 et seq.) by the Federal Communications Commission with respect to any person subject to the provisions of that Act.

(c) EXERCISE OF CERTAIN POWERS.—For the purpose of the exercise by any agency referred to in subsection (b) of its powers under any Act referred to in that subsection, a violation of this Act is deemed to be a violation of a Federal Trade Commission trade regulation rule. In addition to its powers under any provision of law specifically referred to in subsection (b), each of the agencies referred to in that subsection may exercise, for the purpose of enforcing compliance with any requirement imposed under this Act, any other authority conferred on it by law.

(d) ACTIONS BY THE COMMISSION.—The Commission shall prevent any person from violating this Act in the same manner, by the same means, and with the same jurisdiction, powers, and duties as though all applicable terms and provisions of the Federal Trade Commission Act (15 U.S.C. 41 et seq.) were incorporated into and made a part of this Act. Any entity that violates any provision of that subtitle is subject to the penalties and entitled to the privileges and immunities provided in the Federal Trade Commission Act in the same manner, by the same means, and with the same jurisdiction, power, and duties as though all applicable terms and provisions of the Federal Trade Commission Act were incorporated into and made a part of that subtitle.

(e) AVAILABILITY OF CEASE–AND–DESIST ORDERS AND INJUNCTIVE RELIEF WITHOUT SHOWING OF KNOWLEDGE.—Notwithstanding any other provision of this Act, in any proceeding or action pursuant to subsection (a), (b), (c), or (d) of this section to enforce compliance, through an order to cease and desist or an injunction, with section 5(a)(1)(C), section 5(a)(2), clause (ii), (iii), or (iv) of section 5(a)(4)(A), section 5(b)(1)(A), or section 5(b)(3), neither the Commission nor the Federal Communications Commission shall be required to allege or prove the state of mind required by such section or subparagraph.

(f) Enforcement by States—

(1) CIVIL ACTION.—In any case in which the attorney general of a State, or an official or agency of a State, has reason to believe that an interest of the residents of that State has been or is threatened or adversely affected by any person who violates paragraph (1) or (2) of section 5(a), who violates section 5(d), or who engages in a pattern or practice that violates paragraph (3), (4), or (5) of section 5(a), of this Act, the attorney general, official, or agency of the State, as parens patriae, may bring a civil action on behalf of the residents of the State in a district court of the United States of appropriate jurisdiction—
  (A) to enjoin further violation of section 5 of this Act by the defendant; or
  (B) to obtain damages on behalf of residents of the State, in an amount equal to the greater of—
    (i) the actual monetary loss suffered by such residents; or
    (ii) the amount determined under paragraph (3).

(2) AVAILABILITY OF INJUNCTIVE RELIEF WITHOUT SHOWING OF KNOWLEDGE.—Notwithstanding any other provision of this Act, in a civil action under paragraph (1)(A) of this subsection, the attorney general, official, or agency of the State shall not be required to allege or prove the state of mind required by section 5(a)(1)(C), section 5(a)(2), clause (ii), (iii), or (iv) of section 5(a)(4)(A), section 5(b)(1)(A), or section 5(b)(3).

(3) Statutory damages—
  (A) IN GENERAL.—For purposes of paragraph (1)(B)(ii), the amount determined under this paragraph is the amount calculated by multiplying the number of violations (with each separately addressed unlawful message received by or addressed to such residents treated as a separate violation) by up to $250.

(B) LIMITATION.—For any violation of section 5 (other than section 5(a)(1)), the amount determined under subparagraph (A) may not exceed $2,000,000.

(C) AGGRAVATED DAMAGES.—The court may increase a damage award to an amount equal to not more than three times the amount otherwise available under this paragraph if—
   (i) the court determines that the defendant committed the violation willfully and knowingly; or
   (ii) the defendant's unlawful activity included one or more of the aggravating violations set forth in section 5(b).

(D) REDUCTION OF DAMAGES.—In assessing damages under subparagraph (A), the court may consider whether—
   (i) the defendant has established and implemented, with due care, commercially reasonable practices and procedures designed to effectively prevent such violations; or
   (ii) the violation occurred despite commercially reasonable efforts to maintain compliance the practices and procedures to which reference is made in clause (i).

(4) ATTORNEY FEES.—In the case of any successful action under paragraph (1), the court, in its discretion, may award the costs of the action and reasonable attorney fees to the State.

(5) RIGHTS OF FEDERAL REGULATORS.—The State shall serve prior written notice of any action under paragraph (1) upon the Federal Trade Commission or the appropriate Federal regulator determined under subsection (b) and provide the Commission or appropriate Federal regulator with a copy of its complaint, except in any case in which such prior notice is not feasible, in which case the State shall serve such notice immediately upon instituting such action. The Federal Trade Commission or appropriate Federal regulator shall have the right—
   (A) to intervene in the action;
   (B) upon so intervening, to be heard on all matters arising therein;
   (C) to remove the action to the appropriate United States district court; and
   (D) to file petitions for appeal.

(6) CONSTRUCTION.—For purposes of bringing any civil action under paragraph (1), nothing in this Act shall be construed to prevent an attorney general of a State from exercising the powers conferred on the attorney general by the laws of that State to—
   (A) conduct investigations;
   (B) administer oaths or affirmations; or
   (C) compel the attendance of witnesses or the production of documentary and other evidence.

(7) VENUE; SERVICE OF PROCESS.—
   (A) VENUE.—Any action brought under paragraph (1) may be brought in the district court of the United States that meets applicable requirements relating to venue under section 1391 of title 28, United States Code.
   (B) SERVICE OF PROCESS.—In an action brought under paragraph (1), process may be served in any district in which the defendant—
      (i) is an inhabitant; or
      (ii) maintains a physical place of business.

(8) LIMITATION ON STATE ACTION WHILE FEDERAL ACTION IS PENDING.—If the Commission, or other appropriate Federal agency under subsection (b), has instituted a civil action or an administrative action for violation of this Act, no State attorney general, or official or agency of a State, may bring an action under this

subsection during the pendency of that action against any defendant named in the complaint of the Commission or the other agency for any violation of this Act alleged in the complaint.

(9) REQUISITE SCIENTER FOR CERTAIN CIVIL ACTIONS.—Except as provided in section 5(a)(1)(C), section 5(a)(2), clause (ii), (iii), or (iv) of section 5(a)(4)(A), section 5(b)(1)(A), or section 5(b)(3), in a civil action brought by a State attorney general, or an official or agency of a State, to recover monetary damages for a violation of this Act, the court shall not grant the relief sought unless the attorney general, official, or agency establishes that the defendant acted with actual knowledge, or knowledge fairly implied on the basis of objective circumstances, of the act or omission that constitutes the violation.

(g) Action by Provider of Internet Access Service—

(1) ACTION AUTHORIZED.—A provider of Internet access service adversely affected by a violation of section 5(a)(1), 5(b), or 5(d), or a pattern or practice that violates paragraph (2), (3), (4), or (5) of section 5(a), may bring a civil action in any district court of the United States with jurisdiction over the defendant—

  (A) to enjoin further violation by the defendant; or

  (B) to recover damages in an amount equal to the greater of—

    (i) actual monetary loss incurred by the provider of Internet access service as a result of such violation; or

    (ii) the amount determined under paragraph (3).

(2) SPECIAL DEFINITION OF "PROCURE".—In any action brought under paragraph (1), this Act shall be applied as if the definition of the term "procure" in section 3(12) contained, after "behalf" the words "with actual knowledge, or by consciously avoiding knowing, whether such person is engaging, or will engage, in a pattern or practice that violates this Act".

(3) STATUTORY DAMAGES.—

  (A) IN GENERAL.—For purposes of paragraph (1)(B)(ii), the amount determined under this paragraph is the amount calculated by multiplying the number of violations (with each separately addressed unlawful message that is transmitted or attempted to be transmitted over the facilities of the provider of Internet access service, or that is transmitted or attempted to be transmitted to an electronic mail address obtained from the provider of Internet access service in violation of section 5(b)(1)(A)(i), treated as a separate violation) by—

    (i) up to $100, in the case of a violation of section 5(a)(1); or

    (ii) up to $25, in the case of any other violation of section 5.

  (B) LIMITATION.—For any violation of section 5 (other than section 5(a)(1)), the amount determined under subparagraph (A) may not exceed $1,000,000.

  (C) AGGRAVATED DAMAGES.—The court may increase a damage award to an amount equal to not more than three times the amount otherwise available under this paragraph if—

    (i) the court determines that the defendant committed the violation willfully and knowingly; or

    (ii) the defendant's unlawful activity included one or more of the aggravated violations set forth in section 5(b).

  (D) REDUCTION OF DAMAGES.—In assessing damages under subparagraph (A), the court may consider whether—

    (i) the defendant has established and implemented, with due care, commercially reasonable practices and procedures designed to effectively prevent such violations; or

    (ii) the violation occurred despite commercially reasonable efforts to maintain compliance with the practices and procedures to which reference is made in clause (i).

(4) ATTORNEY FEES.—In any action brought pursuant to paragraph (1), the court may, in its discretion, require an undertaking for the payment of the costs of such action, and assess reasonable costs, including reasonable attorneys' fees, against any party.

# EU General Data Protection Regulation (GDPR) (Effective 2018)
## *Regulation (EU) 2016/679 of the European Parliament and of the Council*

Article 1. Subject-matter and objectives

1. This Regulation lays down rules relating to the protection of natural persons with regard to the processing of personal data and rules relating to the free movement of personal data.

2. This Regulation protects fundamental rights and freedoms of natural persons and in particular their right to the protection of personal data.

3. The free movement of personal data within the Union shall be neither restricted nor prohibited for reasons connected with the protection of natural persons with regard to the processing of personal data.

Article 2. Material scope

1. This Regulation applies to the processing of personal data wholly or partly by automated means and to the processing other than by automated means of personal data which form part of a filing system or are intended to form part of a filing system.

2. This Regulation does not apply to the processing of personal data:

> (a) in the course of an activity which falls outside the scope of Union law;

> (b) by the Member States when carrying out activities which fall within the scope of Chapter 2 of Title V of the TEU;

> (c) by a natural person in the course of a purely personal or household activity;

> (d) by competent authorities for the purposes of the prevention, investigation, detection or prosecution of criminal offences or the execution of criminal penalties, including the safeguarding against and the prevention of threats to public security. ***

4. This Regulation shall be without prejudice to the application of Directive 2000/31/EC, in particular of the liability rules of intermediary service providers in Articles 12 to 15 of that Directive.

Article 3. Territorial scope

1. This Regulation applies to the processing of personal data in the context of the activities of an establishment of a controller or a processor in the Union, regardless of whether the processing takes place in the Union or not.

2.  This Regulation applies to the processing of personal data of data subjects who are in the Union by a controller or processor not established in the Union, where the processing activities are related to:

> (a) the offering of goods or services, irrespective of whether a payment of the data subject is required, to such data subjects in the Union; or

> (b) the monitoring of their behaviour as far as their behaviour takes place within the Union.

3.  This Regulation applies to the processing of personal data by a controller not established in the Union, but in a place where Member State law applies by virtue of public international law.

Article 4. Definitions

For the purposes of this Regulation:

(1) 'personal data' means any information relating to an identified or identifiable natural person ('data subject'); an identifiable natural person is one who can be identified, directly or indirectly, in particular by reference to an identifier such as a name, an identification number, location data, an online identifier or to one or more factors specific to the physical, physiological, genetic, mental, economic, cultural or social identity of that natural person;

(2) 'processing' means any operation or set of operations which is performed on personal data or on sets of personal data, whether or not by automated means, such as collection, recording, organisation, structuring, storage, adaptation or alteration, retrieval, consultation, use, disclosure by transmission, dissemination or otherwise making available, alignment or combination, restriction, erasure or destruction;

(3) 'restriction of processing' means the marking of stored personal data with the aim of limiting their processing in the future;

(4) 'profiling' means any form of automated processing of personal data consisting of the use of personal data to evaluate certain personal aspects relating to a natural person, in particular to analyse or predict aspects concerning that natural person's performance at work, economic situation, health, personal preferences, interests, reliability, behaviour, location or movements;

(5) 'pseudonymisation' means the processing of personal data in such a manner that the personal data can no longer be attributed to a specific data subject without the use of additional information, provided that such additional information is kept separately and is subject to technical and organisational measures to ensure that the personal data are not attributed to an identified or identifiable natural person;

(6) 'filing system' means any structured set of personal data which are accessible according to specific criteria, whether centralised, decentralised or dispersed on a functional or geographical basis;

(7) 'controller' means the natural or legal person, public authority, agency or other body which, alone or jointly with others, determines the purposes and means of the processing of personal data; where the purposes and means

of such processing are determined by Union or Member State law, the controller or the specific criteria for its nomination may be provided for by Union or Member State law;

(8) 'processor' means a natural or legal person, public authority, agency or other body which processes personal data on behalf of the controller;

(9) 'recipient' means a natural or legal person, public authority, agency or another body, to which the personal data are disclosed, whether a third party or not. However, public authorities which may receive personal data in the framework of a particular inquiry in accordance with Union or Member State law shall not be regarded as recipients; the processing of those data by those public authorities shall be in compliance with the applicable data protection rules according to the purposes of the processing;

(10) 'third party' means a natural or legal person, public authority, agency or body other than the data subject, controller, processor and persons who, under the direct authority of the controller or processor, are authorised to process personal data;

(11) 'consent' of the data subject means any freely given, specific, informed and unambiguous indication of the data subject's wishes by which he or she, by a statement or by a clear affirmative action, signifies agreement to the processing of personal data relating to him or her;

(12) 'personal data breach' means a breach of security leading to the accidental or unlawful destruction, loss, alteration, unauthorised disclosure of, or access to, personal data transmitted, stored or otherwise processed;

(13) 'genetic data' means personal data relating to the inherited or acquired genetic characteristics of a natural person which give unique information about the physiology or the health of that natural person and which result, in particular, from an analysis of a biological sample from the natural person in question;

(14) 'biometric data' means personal data resulting from specific technical processing relating to the physical, physiological or behavioural characteristics of a natural person, which allow or confirm the unique identification of that natural person, such as facial images or dactyloscopic data;

(15) 'data concerning health' means personal data related to the physical or mental health of a natural person, including the provision of health care services, which reveal information about his or her health status;

(16) 'main establishment' means:

> (a) as regards a controller with establishments in more than one Member State, the place of its central administration in the Union, unless the decisions on the purposes and means of the processing of personal data are taken in another establishment of the controller in the Union and the latter establishment has the power to have such decisions implemented, in which case the establishment having taken such decisions is to be considered to be the main establishment;

(b) as regards a processor with establishments in more than one Member State, the place of its central administration in the Union, or, if the processor has no central administration in the Union, the establishment of the processor in the Union where the main processing activities in the context of the activities of an establishment of the processor take place to the extent that the processor is subject to specific obligations under this Regulation;

(17) 'representative' means a natural or legal person established in the Union who, designated by the controller or processor in writing pursuant to Article 27, represents the controller or processor with regard to their respective obligations under this Regulation;

(18) 'enterprise' means a natural or legal person engaged in an economic activity, irrespective of its legal form, including partnerships or associations regularly engaged in an economic activity;

(19) 'group of undertakings' means a controlling undertaking and its controlled undertakings;

(20) 'binding corporate rules' means personal data protection policies which are adhered to by a controller or processor established on the territory of a Member State for transfers or a set of transfers of personal data to a controller or processor in one or more third countries within a group of undertakings, or group of enterprises engaged in a joint economic activity;

(21) 'supervisory authority' means an independent public authority which is established by a Member State pursuant to Article 51;

(22) 'supervisory authority concerned' means a supervisory authority which is concerned by the processing of personal data because:

(a) the controller or processor is established on the territory of the Member State of that supervisory authority;

(b) data subjects residing in the Member State of that supervisory authority are substantially affected or likely to be substantially affected by the processing; or

(c) a complaint has been lodged with that supervisory authority;

(23) 'cross-border processing' means either:

(a) processing of personal data which takes place in the context of the activities of establishments in more than one Member State of a controller or processor in the Union where the controller or processor is established in more than one Member State; or

(b) processing of personal data which takes place in the context of the activities of a single establishment of a controller or processor in the Union but which substantially affects or is likely to substantially affect data subjects in more than one Member State.

(24) 'relevant and reasoned objection' means an objection to a draft decision as to whether there is an infringement of this Regulation, or whether envisaged action in relation to the controller or processor complies with this Regulation, which clearly demonstrates the significance of the risks posed by the draft decision as regards the fundamental rights and freedoms of data subjects and, where applicable, the free flow of personal data within the Union;

(25) 'information society service' means a service as defined in point (b) of Article 1(1) of Directive (EU) 2015/1535 of the European Parliament and of the Council (19);

(26) 'international organisation' means an organisation and its subordinate bodies governed by public international law, or any other body which is set up by, or on the basis of, an agreement between two or more countries.

## CHAPTER II
### *Principles*

Article 5. Principles relating to processing of personal data

1.  Personal data shall be:

> (a) processed lawfully, fairly and in a transparent manner in relation to the data subject ('lawfulness, fairness and transparency');

> (b) collected for specified, explicit and legitimate purposes and not further processed in a manner that is incompatible with those purposes; further processing for archiving purposes in the public interest, scientific or historical research purposes or statistical purposes shall, in accordance with Article 89(1), not be considered to be incompatible with the initial purposes ('purpose limitation');

> (c) adequate, relevant and limited to what is necessary in relation to the purposes for which they are processed ('data minimisation');

> (d) accurate and, where necessary, kept up to date; every reasonable step must be taken to ensure that personal data that are inaccurate, having regard to the purposes for which they are processed, are erased or rectified without delay ('accuracy');

> (e) kept in a form which permits identification of data subjects for no longer than is necessary for the purposes for which the personal data are processed; personal data may be stored for longer periods insofar as the personal data will be processed solely for archiving purposes in the public interest, scientific or historical research purposes or statistical purposes in accordance with Article 89(1) subject to implementation of the appropriate technical and organisational measures required by this Regulation in order to safeguard the rights and freedoms of the data subject ('storage limitation');

(f) processed in a manner that ensures appropriate security of the personal data, including protection against unauthorised or unlawful processing and against accidental loss, destruction or damage, using appropriate technical or organisational measures ('integrity and confidentiality').

2. The controller shall be responsible for, and be able to demonstrate compliance with, paragraph 1 ('accountability').

Article 6. Lawfulness of processing

1. Processing shall be lawful only if and to the extent that at least one of the following applies:

(a) the data subject has given consent to the processing of his or her personal data for one or more specific purposes;

(b) processing is necessary for the performance of a contract to which the data subject is party or in order to take steps at the request of the data subject prior to entering into a contract;

(c) processing is necessary for compliance with a legal obligation to which the controller is subject;

(d) processing is necessary in order to protect the vital interests of the data subject or of another natural person;

(e) processing is necessary for the performance of a task carried out in the public interest or in the exercise of official authority vested in the controller;

(f) processing is necessary for the purposes of the legitimate interests pursued by the controller or by a third party, except where such interests are overridden by the interests or fundamental rights and freedoms of the data subject which require protection of personal data, in particular where the data subject is a child.

Point (f) of the first subparagraph shall not apply to processing carried out by public authorities in the performance of their tasks.

2. Member States may maintain or introduce more specific provisions to adapt the application of the rules of this Regulation with regard to processing for compliance with points (c) and (e) of paragraph 1 by determining more precisely specific requirements for the processing and other measures to ensure lawful and fair processing including for other specific processing situations as provided for in Chapter IX.

3. The basis for the processing referred to in point (c) and (e) of paragraph 1 shall be laid down by:

(a) Union law; or

(b) Member State law to which the controller is subject.

The purpose of the processing shall be determined in that legal basis or, as regards the processing referred to in point (e) of paragraph 1, shall be necessary for the performance of a task carried out in the public interest or in the exercise of official authority vested in the controller. That legal basis may contain specific provisions to adapt the application of rules of this Regulation, inter alia: the general conditions governing the lawfulness of processing by the controller; the types of data which are subject to the processing; the data subjects concerned; the entities to, and the purposes for which, the personal data may be disclosed; the purpose limitation; storage periods; and processing operations and processing procedures, including measures to ensure lawful and fair processing such as those for other specific processing situations as provided for in Chapter IX. The Union or the Member State law shall meet an objective of public interest and be proportionate to the legitimate aim pursued.

4. Where the processing for a purpose other than that for which the personal data have been collected is not based on the data subject's consent or on a Union or Member State law which constitutes a necessary and proportionate measure in a democratic society to safeguard the objectives referred to in Article 23(1), the controller shall, in order to ascertain whether processing for another purpose is compatible with the purpose for which the personal data are initially collected, take into account, inter alia:

(a) any link between the purposes for which the personal data have been collected and the purposes of the intended further processing;

(b) the context in which the personal data have been collected, in particular regarding the relationship between data subjects and the controller;

(c) the nature of the personal data, in particular whether special categories of personal data are processed, pursuant to Article 9, or whether personal data related to criminal convictions and offences are processed, pursuant to Article 10;

(d) the possible consequences of the intended further processing for data subjects;

(e) the existence of appropriate safeguards, which may include encryption or pseudonymisation.

Article 7. Conditions for consent

1. Where processing is based on consent, the controller shall be able to demonstrate that the data subject has consented to processing of his or her personal data.

2. If the data subject's consent is given in the context of a written declaration which also concerns other matters, the request for consent shall be presented in a manner which is clearly distinguishable from the other matters, in an intelligible and easily accessible form, using clear and plain language. Any part of such a declaration which constitutes an infringement of this Regulation shall not be binding.

3.  The data subject shall have the right to withdraw his or her consent at any time. The withdrawal of consent shall not affect the lawfulness of processing based on consent before its withdrawal. Prior to giving consent, the data subject shall be informed thereof. It shall be as easy to withdraw as to give consent.

4.  When assessing whether consent is freely given, utmost account shall be taken of whether, inter alia, the performance of a contract, including the provision of a service, is conditional on consent to the processing of personal data that is not necessary for the performance of that contract.

Article 8. Conditions applicable to child's consent in relation to information society services

1.  Where point (a) of Article 6(1) applies, in relation to the offer of information society services directly to a child, the processing of the personal data of a child shall be lawful where the child is at least 16 years old. Where the child is below the age of 16 years, such processing shall be lawful only if and to the extent that consent is given or authorised by the holder of parental responsibility over the child.

Member States may provide by law for a lower age for those purposes provided that such lower age is not below 13 years.

2.  The controller shall make reasonable efforts to verify in such cases that consent is given or authorised by the holder of parental responsibility over the child, taking into consideration available technology.

3.  Paragraph 1 shall not affect the general contract law of Member States such as the rules on the validity, formation or effect of a contract in relation to a child.

Article 9. Processing of special categories of personal data

1.  Processing of personal data revealing racial or ethnic origin, political opinions, religious or philosophical beliefs, or trade union membership, and the processing of genetic data, biometric data for the purpose of uniquely identifying a natural person, data concerning health or data concerning a natural person's sex life or sexual orientation shall be prohibited.

2.  Paragraph 1 shall not apply if one of the following applies:

> (a) the data subject has given explicit consent to the processing of those personal data for one or more specified purposes, except where Union or Member State law provide that the prohibition referred to in paragraph 1 may not be lifted by the data subject;

> (b) processing is necessary for the purposes of carrying out the obligations and exercising specific rights of the controller or of the data subject in the field of employment and social security and social protection law in so far as it is authorised by Union or Member State law or a collective agreement pursuant to Member State law providing for appropriate safeguards for the fundamental rights and the interests of the data subject;

(c) processing is necessary to protect the vital interests of the data subject or of another natural person where the data subject is physically or legally incapable of giving consent;

(d) processing is carried out in the course of its legitimate activities with appropriate safeguards by a foundation, association or any other not-for-profit body with a political, philosophical, religious or trade union aim and on condition that the processing relates solely to the members or to former members of the body or to persons who have regular contact with it in connection with its purposes and that the personal data are not disclosed outside that body without the consent of the data subjects;

(e) processing relates to personal data which are manifestly made public by the data subject;

(f) processing is necessary for the establishment, exercise or defence of legal claims or whenever courts are acting in their judicial capacity;

(g) processing is necessary for reasons of substantial public interest, on the basis of Union or Member State law which shall be proportionate to the aim pursued, respect the essence of the right to data protection and provide for suitable and specific measures to safeguard the fundamental rights and the interests of the data subject;

(h) processing is necessary for the purposes of preventive or occupational medicine, for the assessment of the working capacity of the employee, medical diagnosis, the provision of health or social care or treatment or the management of health or social care systems and services on the basis of Union or Member State law or pursuant to contract with a health professional and subject to the conditions and safeguards referred to in paragraph 3;

(i) processing is necessary for reasons of public interest in the area of public health, such as protecting against serious cross-border threats to health or ensuring high standards of quality and safety of health care and of medicinal products or medical devices, on the basis of Union or Member State law which provides for suitable and specific measures to safeguard the rights and freedoms of the data subject, in particular professional secrecy;

(j) processing is necessary for archiving purposes in the public interest, scientific or historical research purposes or statistical purposes in accordance with Article 89(1) based on Union or Member State law which shall be proportionate to the aim pursued, respect the essence of the right to data protection and provide for suitable and specific measures to safeguard the fundamental rights and the interests of the data subject.

3.  Personal data referred to in paragraph 1 may be processed for the purposes referred to in point (h) of paragraph 2 when those data are processed by or under the responsibility of a professional subject to the obligation of professional secrecy under Union or Member State law or rules established by national competent bodies or by another person also subject to an obligation of secrecy under Union or Member State law or rules established by national competent bodies.

4.  Member States may maintain or introduce further conditions, including limitations, with regard to the processing of genetic data, biometric data or data concerning health.

Article 10. Processing of personal data relating to criminal convictions and offences

Processing of personal data relating to criminal convictions and offences or related security measures based on Article 6(1) shall be carried out only under the control of official authority or when the processing is authorised by Union or Member State law providing for appropriate safeguards for the rights and freedoms of data subjects. Any comprehensive register of criminal convictions shall be kept only under the control of official authority.

Article 11. Processing which does not require identification

1.  If the purposes for which a controller processes personal data do not or do no longer require the identification of a data subject by the controller, the controller shall not be obliged to maintain, acquire or process additional information in order to identify the data subject for the sole purpose of complying with this Regulation.

2.  Where, in cases referred to in paragraph 1 of this Article, the controller is able to demonstrate that it is not in a position to identify the data subject, the controller shall inform the data subject accordingly, if possible. In such cases, Articles 15 to 20 shall not apply except where the data subject, for the purpose of exercising his or her rights under those articles, provides additional information enabling his or her identification.

## CHAPTER III
### Rights of the data subject

Section 1. Transparency and modalities

Article 12. Transparent information, communication and modalities for the exercise of the rights of the data subject

1.  The controller shall take appropriate measures to provide any information referred to in Articles 13 and 14 and any communication under Articles 15 to 22 and 34 relating to processing to the data subject in a concise, transparent, intelligible and easily accessible form, using clear and plain language, in particular for any information addressed specifically to a child. The information shall be provided in writing, or by other means, including, where appropriate, by electronic means. When requested by the data subject, the information may be provided orally, provided that the identity of the data subject is proven by other means.

2.  The controller shall facilitate the exercise of data subject rights under Articles 15 to 22. In the cases referred to in Article 11(2), the controller shall not refuse to act on the request of the data subject for exercising his or her rights under Articles 15 to 22, unless the controller demonstrates that it is not in a position to identify the data subject.

3.  The controller shall provide information on action taken on a request under Articles 15 to 22 to the data subject without undue delay and in any event within one month of receipt of the request. That period may be

extended by two further months where necessary, taking into account the complexity and number of the requests. The controller shall inform the data subject of any such extension within one month of receipt of the request, together with the reasons for the delay. Where the data subject makes the request by electronic form means, the information shall be provided by electronic means where possible, unless otherwise requested by the data subject.

4.  If the controller does not take action on the request of the data subject, the controller shall inform the data subject without delay and at the latest within one month of receipt of the request of the reasons for not taking action and on the possibility of lodging a complaint with a supervisory authority and seeking a judicial remedy.

5.  Information provided under Articles 13 and 14 and any communication and any actions taken under Articles 15 to 22 and 34 shall be provided free of charge. Where requests from a data subject are manifestly unfounded or excessive, in particular because of their repetitive character, the controller may either:

> (a) charge a reasonable fee taking into account the administrative costs of providing the information or communication or taking the action requested; or

> (b) refuse to act on the request.

The controller shall bear the burden of demonstrating the manifestly unfounded or excessive character of the request.

6.  Without prejudice to Article 11, where the controller has reasonable doubts concerning the identity of the natural person making the request referred to in Articles 15 to 21, the controller may request the provision of additional information necessary to confirm the identity of the data subject.

7.  The information to be provided to data subjects pursuant to Articles 13 and 14 may be provided in combination with standardised icons in order to give in an easily visible, intelligible and clearly legible manner a meaningful overview of the intended processing. Where the icons are presented electronically they shall be machine-readable.

8.  The Commission shall be empowered to adopt delegated acts in accordance with Article 92 for the purpose of determining the information to be presented by the icons and the procedures for providing standardised icons.

Section 2. Information and access to personal data

Article 13. Information to be provided where personal data are collected from the data subject

1.  Where personal data relating to a data subject are collected from the data subject, the controller shall, at the time when personal data are obtained, provide the data subject with all of the following information:

> (a) the identity and the contact details of the controller and, where applicable, of the controller's representative;

(b) the contact details of the data protection officer, where applicable;

(c) the purposes of the processing for which the personal data are intended as well as the legal basis for the processing;

(d) where the processing is based on point (f) of Article 6(1), the legitimate interests pursued by the controller or by a third party;

(e) the recipients or categories of recipients of the personal data, if any;

(f) where applicable, the fact that the controller intends to transfer personal data to a third country or international organisation and the existence or absence of an adequacy decision by the Commission, or in the case of transfers referred to in Article 46 or 47, or the second subparagraph of Article 49(1), reference to the appropriate or suitable safeguards and the means by which to obtain a copy of them or where they have been made available.

2.  In addition to the information referred to in paragraph 1, the controller shall, at the time when personal data are obtained, provide the data subject with the following further information necessary to ensure fair and transparent processing:

(a) the period for which the personal data will be stored, or if that is not possible, the criteria used to determine that period;

(b) the existence of the right to request from the controller access to and rectification or erasure of personal data or restriction of processing concerning the data subject or to object to processing as well as the right to data portability;

(c) where the processing is based on point (a) of Article 6(1) or point (a) of Article 9(2), the existence of the right to withdraw consent at any time, without affecting the lawfulness of processing based on consent before its withdrawal;

(d) the right to lodge a complaint with a supervisory authority;

(e) whether the provision of personal data is a statutory or contractual requirement, or a requirement necessary to enter into a contract, as well as whether the data subject is obliged to provide the personal data and of the possible consequences of failure to provide such data;

(f) the existence of automated decision-making, including profiling, referred to in Article 22(1) and (4) and, at least in those cases, meaningful information about the logic involved, as well as the significance and the envisaged consequences of such processing for the data subject.

3. Where the controller intends to further process the personal data for a purpose other than that for which the personal data were collected, the controller shall provide the data subject prior to that further processing with information on that other purpose and with any relevant further information as referred to in paragraph 2.

4. Paragraphs 1, 2 and 3 shall not apply where and insofar as the data subject already has the information.

Article 14. Information to be provided where personal data have not been obtained from the data subject

1. Where personal data have not been obtained from the data subject, the controller shall provide the data subject with the following information:

> (a) the identity and the contact details of the controller and, where applicable, of the controller's representative;

> (b) the contact details of the data protection officer, where applicable;

> (c) the purposes of the processing for which the personal data are intended as well as the legal basis for the processing;

> (d) the categories of personal data concerned;

> (e) the recipients or categories of recipients of the personal data, if any;

> (f) where applicable, that the controller intends to transfer personal data to a recipient in a third country or international organisation and the existence or absence of an adequacy decision by the Commission, or in the case of transfers referred to in Article 46 or 47, or the second subparagraph of Article 49(1), reference to the appropriate or suitable safeguards and the means to obtain a copy of them or where they have been made available.

2. In addition to the information referred to in paragraph 1, the controller shall provide the data subject with the following information necessary to ensure fair and transparent processing in respect of the data subject:

> (a) the period for which the personal data will be stored, or if that is not possible, the criteria used to determine that period;

> (b) where the processing is based on point (f) of Article 6(1), the legitimate interests pursued by the controller or by a third party;

> (c) the existence of the right to request from the controller access to and rectification or erasure of personal data or restriction of processing concerning the data subject and to object to processing as well as the right to data portability;

(d) where processing is based on point (a) of Article 6(1) or point (a) of Article 9(2), the existence of the right to withdraw consent at any time, without affecting the lawfulness of processing based on consent before its withdrawal;

(e) the right to lodge a complaint with a supervisory authority;

(f) from which source the personal data originate, and if applicable, whether it came from publicly accessible sources;

(g) the existence of automated decision-making, including profiling, referred to in Article 22(1) and (4) and, at least in those cases, meaningful information about the logic involved, as well as the significance and the envisaged consequences of such processing for the data subject.

3.  The controller shall provide the information referred to in paragraphs 1 and 2:

(a) within a reasonable period after obtaining the personal data, but at the latest within one month, having regard to the specific circumstances in which the personal data are processed;

(b) if the personal data are to be used for communication with the data subject, at the latest at the time of the first communication to that data subject; or

(c) if a disclosure to another recipient is envisaged, at the latest when the personal data are first disclosed.

4.  Where the controller intends to further process the personal data for a purpose other than that for which the personal data were obtained, the controller shall provide the data subject prior to that further processing with information on that other purpose and with any relevant further information as referred to in paragraph 2.

5.  Paragraphs 1 to 4 shall not apply where and insofar as:

(a) the data subject already has the information;

(b) the provision of such information proves impossible or would involve a disproportionate effort, in particular for processing for archiving purposes in the public interest, scientific or historical research purposes or statistical purposes, subject to the conditions and safeguards referred to in Article 89(1) or in so far as the obligation referred to in paragraph 1 of this Article is likely to render impossible or seriously impair the achievement of the objectives of that processing. In such cases the controller shall take appropriate measures to protect the data subject's rights and freedoms and legitimate interests, including making the information publicly available;

(c) obtaining or disclosure is expressly laid down by Union or Member State law to which the controller is subject and which provides appropriate measures to protect the data subject's legitimate interests; or

(d) where the personal data must remain confidential subject to an obligation of professional secrecy regulated by Union or Member State law, including a statutory obligation of secrecy.

Article 15. Right of access by the data subject

1.  The data subject shall have the right to obtain from the controller confirmation as to whether or not personal data concerning him or her are being processed, and, where that is the case, access to the personal data and the following information:

(a) the purposes of the processing;

(b) the categories of personal data concerned;

(c) the recipients or categories of recipient to whom the personal data have been or will be disclosed, in particular recipients in third countries or international organisations;

(d) where possible, the envisaged period for which the personal data will be stored, or, if not possible, the criteria used to determine that period;

(e) the existence of the right to request from the controller rectification or erasure of personal data or restriction of processing of personal data concerning the data subject or to object to such processing;

(f) the right to lodge a complaint with a supervisory authority;

(g) where the personal data are not collected from the data subject, any available information as to their source;

(h) the existence of automated decision-making, including profiling, referred to in Article 22(1) and (4) and, at least in those cases, meaningful information about the logic involved, as well as the significance and the envisaged consequences of such processing for the data subject.

2.  Where personal data are transferred to a third country or to an international organisation, the data subject shall have the right to be informed of the appropriate safeguards pursuant to Article 46 relating to the transfer.

3.  The controller shall provide a copy of the personal data undergoing processing. For any further copies requested by the data subject, the controller may charge a reasonable fee based on administrative costs. Where the data subject makes the request by electronic means, and unless otherwise requested by the data subject, the information shall be provided in a commonly used electronic form.

4.  The right to obtain a copy referred to in paragraph 3 shall not adversely affect the rights and freedoms of others.

*Section 3. Rectification and erasure*

Article 16. Right to rectification

The data subject shall have the right to obtain from the controller without undue delay the rectification of inaccurate personal data concerning him or her. Taking into account the purposes of the processing, the data subject shall have the right to have incomplete personal data completed, including by means of providing a supplementary statement.

Article 17. Right to erasure ('right to be forgotten')

1. The data subject shall have the right to obtain from the controller the erasure of personal data concerning him or her without undue delay and the controller shall have the obligation to erase personal data without undue delay where one of the following grounds applies:

(a) the personal data are no longer necessary in relation to the purposes for which they were collected or otherwise processed;

(b) the data subject withdraws consent on which the processing is based according to point (a) of Article 6(1), or point (a) of Article 9(2), and where there is no other legal ground for the processing;

(c) the data subject objects to the processing pursuant to Article 21(1) and there are no overriding legitimate grounds for the processing, or the data subject objects to the processing pursuant to Article 21(2);

(d) the personal data have been unlawfully processed;

(e) the personal data have to be erased for compliance with a legal obligation in Union or Member State law to which the controller is subject;

(f) the personal data have been collected in relation to the offer of information society services referred to in Article 8(1).

2. Where the controller has made the personal data public and is obliged pursuant to paragraph 1 to erase the personal data, the controller, taking account of available technology and the cost of implementation, shall take reasonable steps, including technical measures, to inform controllers which are processing the personal data that the data subject has requested the erasure by such controllers of any links to, or copy or replication of, those personal data.

3. Paragraphs 1 and 2 shall not apply to the extent that processing is necessary:

(a) for exercising the right of freedom of expression and information;

(b) for compliance with a legal obligation which requires processing by Union or Member State law to which the controller is subject or for the performance of a task carried out in the public interest or in the exercise of official authority vested in the controller;

(c) for reasons of public interest in the area of public health in accordance with points (h) and (i) of Article 9(2) as well as Article 9(3);

(d) for archiving purposes in the public interest, scientific or historical research purposes or statistical purposes in accordance with Article 89(1) in so far as the right referred to in paragraph 1 is likely to render impossible or seriously impair the achievement of the objectives of that processing; or

(e) for the establishment, exercise or defence of legal claims.

Article 18. Right to restriction of processing

1.  The data subject shall have the right to obtain from the controller restriction of processing where one of the following applies:

(a) the accuracy of the personal data is contested by the data subject, for a period enabling the controller to verify the accuracy of the personal data;

(b) the processing is unlawful and the data subject opposes the erasure of the personal data and requests the restriction of their use instead;

(c) the controller no longer needs the personal data for the purposes of the processing, but they are required by the data subject for the establishment, exercise or defence of legal claims;

(d) the data subject has objected to processing pursuant to Article 21(1) pending the verification whether the legitimate grounds of the controller override those of the data subject.

2.  Where processing has been restricted under paragraph 1, such personal data shall, with the exception of storage, only be processed with the data subject's consent or for the establishment, exercise or defence of legal claims or for the protection of the rights of another natural or legal person or for reasons of important public interest of the Union or of a Member State.

3.  A data subject who has obtained restriction of processing pursuant to paragraph 1 shall be informed by the controller before the restriction of processing is lifted.

Article 19. Notification obligation regarding rectification or erasure of personal data or restriction of processing

The controller shall communicate any rectification or erasure of personal data or restriction of processing carried out in accordance with Article 16, Article 17(1) and Article 18 to each recipient to whom the personal data have been disclosed, unless this proves impossible or involves disproportionate effort. The controller shall inform the data subject about those recipients if the data subject requests it.

Article 20. Right to data portability

1.   The data subject shall have the right to receive the personal data concerning him or her, which he or she has provided to a controller, in a structured, commonly used and machine-readable format and have the right to transmit those data to another controller without hindrance from the controller to which the personal data have been provided, where:

>    (a) the processing is based on consent pursuant to point (a) of Article 6(1) or point (a) of Article 9(2) or on a contract pursuant to point (b) of Article 6(1); and

>    (b) the processing is carried out by automated means.

2.   In exercising his or her right to data portability pursuant to paragraph 1, the data subject shall have the right to have the personal data transmitted directly from one controller to another, where technically feasible.

3.   The exercise of the right referred to in paragraph 1 of this Article shall be without prejudice to Article 17. That right shall not apply to processing necessary for the performance of a task carried out in the public interest or in the exercise of official authority vested in the controller.

4.   The right referred to in paragraph 1 shall not adversely affect the rights and freedoms of others.

## Section 4. Right to object and automated individual decision-making

Article 21. Right to object

1.   The data subject shall have the right to object, on grounds relating to his or her particular situation, at any time to processing of personal data concerning him or her which is based on point (e) or (f) of Article 6(1), including profiling based on those provisions. The controller shall no longer process the personal data unless the controller demonstrates compelling legitimate grounds for the processing which override the interests, rights and freedoms of the data subject or for the establishment, exercise or defence of legal claims.

2.   Where personal data are processed for direct marketing purposes, the data subject shall have the right to object at any time to processing of personal data concerning him or her for such marketing, which includes profiling to the extent that it is related to such direct marketing.

3.   Where the data subject objects to processing for direct marketing purposes, the personal data shall no longer be processed for such purposes.

4.  At the latest at the time of the first communication with the data subject, the right referred to in paragraphs 1 and 2 shall be explicitly brought to the attention of the data subject and shall be presented clearly and separately from any other information.

5.  In the context of the use of information society services, and notwithstanding Directive 2002/58/EC, the data subject may exercise his or her right to object by automated means using technical specifications.

6.  Where personal data are processed for scientific or historical research purposes or statistical purposes pursuant to Article 89(1), the data subject, on grounds relating to his or her particular situation, shall have the right to object to processing of personal data concerning him or her, unless the processing is necessary for the performance of a task carried out for reasons of public interest.

Article 22. Automated individual decision-making, including profiling

1.  The data subject shall have the right not to be subject to a decision based solely on automated processing, including profiling, which produces legal effects concerning him or her or similarly significantly affects him or her.

2.  Paragraph 1 shall not apply if the decision:

> (a) is necessary for entering into, or performance of, a contract between the data subject and a data controller;
>
> (b) is authorised by Union or Member State law to which the controller is subject and which also lays down suitable measures to safeguard the data subject's rights and freedoms and legitimate interests; or
>
> (c) is based on the data subject's explicit consent.

3.  In the cases referred to in points (a) and (c) of paragraph 2, the data controller shall implement suitable measures to safeguard the data subject's rights and freedoms and legitimate interests, at least the right to obtain human intervention on the part of the controller, to express his or her point of view and to contest the decision.

4.  Decisions referred to in paragraph 2 shall not be based on special categories of personal data referred to in Article 9(1), unless point (a) or (g) of Article 9(2) applies and suitable measures to safeguard the data subject's rights and freedoms and legitimate interests are in place.

*Section 5. Restrictions*

Article 23. Restrictions

1.  Union or Member State law to which the data controller or processor is subject may restrict by way of a legislative measure the scope of the obligations and rights provided for in Articles 12 to 22 and Article 34, as well as Article 5 in so far as its provisions correspond to the rights and obligations provided for in Articles 12 to 22,

when such a restriction respects the essence of the fundamental rights and freedoms and is a necessary and proportionate measure in a democratic society to safeguard:

>    (a) national security;

>    (b) defence;

>    (c) public security;

>    (d) the prevention, investigation, detection or prosecution of criminal offences or the execution of criminal penalties, including the safeguarding against and the prevention of threats to public security;

>    (e) other important objectives of general public interest of the Union or of a Member State, in particular an important economic or financial interest of the Union or of a Member State, including monetary, budgetary and taxation a matters, public health and social security;

>    (f) the protection of judicial independence and judicial proceedings;

>    (g) the prevention, investigation, detection and prosecution of breaches of ethics for regulated professions;

>    (h) a monitoring, inspection or regulatory function connected, even occasionally, to the exercise of official authority in the cases referred to in points (a) to (e) and (g);

>    (i) the protection of the data subject or the rights and freedoms of others;

>    (j) the enforcement of civil law claims.

2.  In particular, any legislative measure referred to in paragraph 1 shall contain specific provisions at least, where relevant, as to:

(a) the purposes of the processing or categories of processing;

(b) the categories of personal data;

(c) the scope of the restrictions introduced;

(d) the safeguards to prevent abuse or unlawful access or transfer;

(e) the specification of the controller or categories of controllers;

(f) the storage periods and the applicable safeguards taking into account the nature, scope and purposes of the processing or categories of processing;

(g) the risks to the rights and freedoms of data subjects; and

(h) the right of data subjects to be informed about the restriction, unless that may be prejudicial to the purpose of the restriction.

CHAPTER IV
Controller and processor

Section 1. General obligations

Article 24. Responsibility of the controller

1.  Taking into account the nature, scope, context and purposes of processing as well as the risks of varying likelihood and severity for the rights and freedoms of natural persons, the controller shall implement appropriate technical and organisational measures to ensure and to be able to demonstrate that processing is performed in accordance with this Regulation. Those measures shall be reviewed and updated where necessary.

2.  Where proportionate in relation to processing activities, the measures referred to in paragraph 1 shall include the implementation of appropriate data protection policies by the controller.

3.  Adherence to approved codes of conduct as referred to in Article 40 or approved certification mechanisms as referred to in Article 42 may be used as an element by which to demonstrate compliance with the obligations of the controller.

Article 25. Data protection by design and by default

1.  Taking into account the state of the art, the cost of implementation and the nature, scope, context and purposes of processing as well as the risks of varying likelihood and severity for rights and freedoms of natural persons posed by the processing, the controller shall, both at the time of the determination of the means for processing and at the time of the processing itself, implement appropriate technical and organisational measures, such as pseudonymisation, which are designed to implement data-protection principles, such as data minimisation, in an effective manner and to integrate the necessary safeguards into the processing in order to meet the requirements of this Regulation and protect the rights of data subjects.

2.  The controller shall implement appropriate technical and organisational measures for ensuring that, by default, only personal data which are necessary for each specific purpose of the processing are processed. That obligation applies to the amount of personal data collected, the extent of their processing, the period of their storage and their accessibility. In particular, such measures shall ensure that by default personal data are not made accessible without the individual's intervention to an indefinite number of natural persons.

3.  An approved certification mechanism pursuant to Article 42 may be used as an element to demonstrate compliance with the requirements set out in paragraphs 1 and 2 of this Article.

Article 26. Joint controllers

1.  Where two or more controllers jointly determine the purposes and means of processing, they shall be joint controllers. They shall in a transparent manner determine their respective responsibilities for compliance with the obligations under this Regulation, in particular as regards the exercising of the rights of the data subject and their respective duties to provide the information referred to in Articles 13 and 14, by means of an arrangement between them unless, and in so far as, the respective responsibilities of the controllers are determined by Union or Member State law to which the controllers are subject. The arrangement may designate a contact point for data subjects.

2.  The arrangement referred to in paragraph 1 shall duly reflect the respective roles and relationships of the joint controllers vis-à-vis the data subjects. The essence of the arrangement shall be made available to the data subject.

3.  Irrespective of the terms of the arrangement referred to in paragraph 1, the data subject may exercise his or her rights under this Regulation in respect of and against each of the controllers.

Article 27. Representatives of controllers or processors not established in the Union

1.  Where Article 3(2) applies, the controller or the processor shall designate in writing a representative in the Union.

2.  The obligation laid down in paragraph 1 of this Article shall not apply to:

> (a) processing which is occasional, does not include, on a large scale, processing of special categories of data as referred to in Article 9(1) or processing of personal data relating to criminal convictions and offences referred to in Article 10, and is unlikely to result in a risk to the rights and freedoms of natural persons, taking into account the nature, context, scope and purposes of the processing; or

> (b) a public authority or body.

3.  The representative shall be established in one of the Member States where the data subjects, whose personal data are processed in relation to the offering of goods or services to them, or whose behaviour is monitored, are.

4.  The representative shall be mandated by the controller or processor to be addressed in addition to or instead of the controller or the processor by, in particular, supervisory authorities and data subjects, on all issues related to processing, for the purposes of ensuring compliance with this Regulation.

5.  The designation of a representative by the controller or processor shall be without prejudice to legal actions which could be initiated against the controller or the processor themselves.

Article 28. Processor

1.  Where processing is to be carried out on behalf of a controller, the controller shall use only processors providing sufficient guarantees to implement appropriate technical and organisational measures in such a manner that processing will meet the requirements of this Regulation and ensure the protection of the rights of the data subject.

2.  The processor shall not engage another processor without prior specific or general written authorisation of the controller. In the case of general written authorisation, the processor shall inform the controller of any intended changes concerning the addition or replacement of other processors, thereby giving the controller the opportunity to object to such changes.

3.  Processing by a processor shall be governed by a contract or other legal act under Union or Member State law, that is binding on the processor with regard to the controller and that sets out the subject-matter and duration of the processing, the nature and purpose of the processing, the type of personal data and categories of data subjects and the obligations and rights of the controller. That contract or other legal act shall stipulate, in particular, that the processor:

> (a) processes the personal data only on documented instructions from the controller, including with regard to transfers of personal data to a third country or an international organisation, unless required to do so by Union or Member State law to which the processor is subject; in such a case, the processor shall inform the controller of that legal requirement before processing, unless that law prohibits such information on important grounds of public interest;

> (b) ensures that persons authorised to process the personal data have committed themselves to confidentiality or are under an appropriate statutory obligation of confidentiality;

> (c) takes all measures required pursuant to Article 32;

> (d) respects the conditions referred to in paragraphs 2 and 4 for engaging another processor;

> (e) taking into account the nature of the processing, assists the controller by appropriate technical and organisational measures, insofar as this is possible, for the fulfilment of the controller's obligation to respond to requests for exercising the data subject's rights laid down in Chapter III;

> (f) assists the controller in ensuring compliance with the obligations pursuant to Articles 32 to 36 taking into account the nature of processing and the information available to the processor;

> (g) at the choice of the controller, deletes or returns all the personal data to the controller after the end of the provision of services relating to processing, and deletes existing copies unless Union or Member State law requires storage of the personal data;

> (h) makes available to the controller all information necessary to demonstrate compliance with the obligations laid down in this Article and allow for and contribute to audits, including inspections, conducted by the controller or another auditor mandated by the controller.

With regard to point (h) of the first subparagraph, the processor shall immediately inform the controller if, in its opinion, an instruction infringes this Regulation or other Union or Member State data protection provisions.

4.  Where a processor engages another processor for carrying out specific processing activities on behalf of the controller, the same data protection obligations as set out in the contract or other legal act between the controller and the processor as referred to in paragraph 3 shall be imposed on that other processor by way of a contract or other legal act under Union or Member State law, in particular providing sufficient guarantees to implement appropriate technical and organisational measures in such a manner that the processing will meet the requirements of this Regulation. Where that other processor fails to fulfil its data protection obligations, the initial processor shall remain fully liable to the controller for the performance of that other processor's obligations.

5.  Adherence of a processor to an approved code of conduct as referred to in Article 40 or an approved certification mechanism as referred to in Article 42 may be used as an element by which to demonstrate sufficient guarantees as referred to in paragraphs 1 and 4 of this Article.

6.  Without prejudice to an individual contract between the controller and the processor, the contract or the other legal act referred to in paragraphs 3 and 4 of this Article may be based, in whole or in part, on standard contractual clauses referred to in paragraphs 7 and 8 of this Article, including when they are part of a certification granted to the controller or processor pursuant to Articles 42 and 43.

7.  The Commission may lay down standard contractual clauses for the matters referred to in paragraph 3 and 4 of this Article and in accordance with the examination procedure referred to in Article 93(2).

8.  A supervisory authority may adopt standard contractual clauses for the matters referred to in paragraph 3 and 4 of this Article and in accordance with the consistency mechanism referred to in Article 63.

9.  The contract or the other legal act referred to in paragraphs 3 and 4 shall be in writing, including in electronic form.

10.  Without prejudice to Articles 82, 83 and 84, if a processor infringes this Regulation by determining the purposes and means of processing, the processor shall be considered to be a controller in respect of that processing.

\*\*\*

*Section 2. Security of personal data*

Article 32. Security of processing

1.  Taking into account the state of the art, the costs of implementation and the nature, scope, context and purposes of processing as well as the risk of varying likelihood and severity for the rights and freedoms of natural

persons, the controller and the processor shall implement appropriate technical and organisational measures to ensure a level of security appropriate to the risk, including inter alia as appropriate:

> (a) the pseudonymisation and encryption of personal data;

> (b) the ability to ensure the ongoing confidentiality, integrity, availability and resilience of processing systems and services;

> (c) the ability to restore the availability and access to personal data in a timely manner in the event of a physical or technical incident;

> (d) a process for regularly testing, assessing and evaluating the effectiveness of technical and organisational measures for ensuring the security of the processing.

2. In assessing the appropriate level of security account shall be taken in particular of the risks that are presented by processing, in particular from accidental or unlawful destruction, loss, alteration, unauthorised disclosure of, or access to personal data transmitted, stored or otherwise processed.

3. Adherence to an approved code of conduct as referred to in Article 40 or an approved certification mechanism as referred to in Article 42 may be used as an element by which to demonstrate compliance with the requirements set out in paragraph 1 of this Article.

4. The controller and processor shall take steps to ensure that any natural person acting under the authority of the controller or the processor who has access to personal data does not process them except on instructions from the controller, unless he or she is required to do so by Union or Member State law.

Article 33. Notification of a personal data breach to the supervisory authority

1. In the case of a personal data breach, the controller shall without undue delay and, where feasible, not later than 72 hours after having become aware of it, notify the personal data breach to the supervisory authority competent in accordance with Article 55, unless the personal data breach is unlikely to result in a risk to the rights and freedoms of natural persons. Where the notification to the supervisory authority is not made within 72 hours, it shall be accompanied by reasons for the delay.

2. The processor shall notify the controller without undue delay after becoming aware of a personal data breach.

3. The notification referred to in paragraph 1 shall at least:

> (a) describe the nature of the personal data breach including where possible, the categories and approximate number of data subjects concerned and the categories and approximate number of personal data records concerned;

(b) communicate the name and contact details of the data protection officer or other contact point where more information can be obtained;

(c) describe the likely consequences of the personal data breach;

(d) describe the measures taken or proposed to be taken by the controller to address the personal data breach, including, where appropriate, measures to mitigate its possible adverse effects.

4. Where, and in so far as, it is not possible to provide the information at the same time, the information may be provided in phases without undue further delay.

5. The controller shall document any personal data breaches, comprising the facts relating to the personal data breach, its effects and the remedial action taken. That documentation shall enable the supervisory authority to verify compliance with this Article.

Article 34. Communication of a personal data breach to the data subject

1. When the personal data breach is likely to result in a high risk to the rights and freedoms of natural persons, the controller shall communicate the personal data breach to the data subject without undue delay.

2. The communication to the data subject referred to in paragraph 1 of this Article shall describe in clear and plain language the nature of the personal data breach and contain at least the information and measures referred to in points (b), (c) and (d) of Article 33(3).

3. The communication to the data subject referred to in paragraph 1 shall not be required if any of the following conditions are met:

(a) the controller has implemented appropriate technical and organisational protection measures, and those measures were applied to the personal data affected by the personal data breach, in particular those that render the personal data unintelligible to any person who is not authorised to access it, such as encryption;

(b) the controller has taken subsequent measures which ensure that the high risk to the rights and freedoms of data subjects referred to in paragraph 1 is no longer likely to materialise;

(c) it would involve disproportionate effort. In such a case, there shall instead be a public communication or similar measure whereby the data subjects are informed in an equally effective manner.

4. If the controller has not already communicated the personal data breach to the data subject, the supervisory authority, having considered the likelihood of the personal data breach resulting in a high risk, may require it to do so or may decide that any of the conditions referred to in paragraph 3 are met.

*Section 3. Data protection impact assessment and prior consultation*

Article 35. Data protection impact assessment

1.  Where a type of processing in particular using new technologies, and taking into account the nature, scope, context and purposes of the processing, is likely to result in a high risk to the rights and freedoms of natural persons, the controller shall, prior to the processing, carry out an assessment of the impact of the envisaged processing operations on the protection of personal data. A single assessment may address a set of similar processing operations that present similar high risks.

2.  The controller shall seek the advice of the data protection officer, where designated, when carrying out a data protection impact assessment.

3.  A data protection impact assessment referred to in paragraph 1 shall in particular be required in the case of:

> (a) a systematic and extensive evaluation of personal aspects relating to natural persons which is based on automated processing, including profiling, and on which decisions are based that produce legal effects concerning the natural person or similarly significantly affect the natural person;

> (b) processing on a large scale of special categories of data referred to in Article 9(1), or of personal data relating to criminal convictions and offences referred to in Article 10; or

> (c) a systematic monitoring of a publicly accessible area on a large scale.

4.  The supervisory authority shall establish and make public a list of the kind of processing operations which are subject to the requirement for a data protection impact assessment pursuant to paragraph 1. The supervisory authority shall communicate those lists to the Board referred to in Article 68.

5.  The supervisory authority may also establish and make public a list of the kind of processing operations for which no data protection impact assessment is required. The supervisory authority shall communicate those lists to the Board.

6.  Prior to the adoption of the lists referred to in paragraphs 4 and 5, the competent supervisory authority shall apply the consistency mechanism referred to in Article 63 where such lists involve processing activities which are related to the offering of goods or services to data subjects or to the monitoring of their behaviour in several Member States, or may substantially affect the free movement of personal data within the Union.

7.  The assessment shall contain at least:

> (a) a systematic description of the envisaged processing operations and the purposes of the processing, including, where applicable, the legitimate interest pursued by the controller;

(b) an assessment of the necessity and proportionality of the processing operations in relation to the purposes;

(c) an assessment of the risks to the rights and freedoms of data subjects referred to in paragraph 1; and

(d) the measures envisaged to address the risks, including safeguards, security measures and mechanisms to ensure the protection of personal data and to demonstrate compliance with this Regulation taking into account the rights and legitimate interests of data subjects and other persons concerned.

8.   Compliance with approved codes of conduct referred to in Article 40 by the relevant controllers or processors shall be taken into due account in assessing the impact of the processing operations performed by such controllers or processors, in particular for the purposes of a data protection impact assessment.

9.   Where appropriate, the controller shall seek the views of data subjects or their representatives on the intended processing, without prejudice to the protection of commercial or public interests or the security of processing operations.

10.   Where processing pursuant to point (c) or (e) of Article 6(1) has a legal basis in Union law or in the law of the Member State to which the controller is subject, that law regulates the specific processing operation or set of operations in question, and a data protection impact assessment has already been carried out as part of a general impact assessment in the context of the adoption of that legal basis, paragraphs 1 to 7 shall not apply unless Member States deem it to be necessary to carry out such an assessment prior to processing activities.

11.   Where necessary, the controller shall carry out a review to assess if processing is performed in accordance with the data protection impact assessment at least when there is a change of the risk represented by processing operations.

Article 36. Prior consultation

1.   The controller shall consult the supervisory authority prior to processing where a data protection impact assessment under Article 35 indicates that the processing would result in a high risk in the absence of measures taken by the controller to mitigate the risk.

2.   Where the supervisory authority is of the opinion that the intended processing referred to in paragraph 1 would infringe this Regulation, in particular where the controller has insufficiently identified or mitigated the risk, the supervisory authority shall, within period of up to eight weeks of receipt of the request for consultation, provide written advice to the controller and, where applicable to the processor, and may use any of its powers referred to in Article 58. That period may be extended by six weeks, taking into account the complexity of the intended processing. The supervisory authority shall inform the controller and, where applicable, the processor, of any such extension within one month of receipt of the request for consultation together with the reasons for the delay. Those periods may be suspended until the supervisory authority has obtained information it has requested for the purposes of the consultation.

3.  When consulting the supervisory authority pursuant to paragraph 1, the controller shall provide the supervisory authority with:

> (a) where applicable, the respective responsibilities of the controller, joint controllers and processors involved in the processing, in particular for processing within a group of undertakings;
>
> (b) the purposes and means of the intended processing;
>
> (c) the measures and safeguards provided to protect the rights and freedoms of data subjects pursuant to this Regulation;
>
> (d) where applicable, the contact details of the data protection officer;
>
> (e) the data protection impact assessment provided for in Article 35; and
>
> (f) any other information requested by the supervisory authority.

4.  Member States shall consult the supervisory authority during the preparation of a proposal for a legislative measure to be adopted by a national parliament, or of a regulatory measure based on such a legislative measure, which relates to processing.

5.  Notwithstanding paragraph 1, Member State law may require controllers to consult with, and obtain prior authorisation from, the supervisory authority in relation to processing by a controller for the performance of a task carried out by the controller in the public interest, including processing in relation to social protection and public health.

*Section 4. Data protection officer*

Article 37. Designation of the data protection officer

1.  The controller and the processor shall designate a data protection officer in any case where:

> (a) the processing is carried out by a public authority or body, except for courts acting in their judicial capacity;
>
> (b) the core activities of the controller or the processor consist of processing operations which, by virtue of their nature, their scope and/or their purposes, require regular and systematic monitoring of data subjects on a large scale; or
>
> (c) the core activities of the controller or the processor consist of processing on a large scale of special categories of data pursuant to Article 9 and personal data relating to criminal convictions and offences referred to in Article 10.

2.  A group of undertakings may appoint a single data protection officer provided that a data protection officer is easily accessible from each establishment.

3.  Where the controller or the processor is a public authority or body, a single data protection officer may be designated for several such authorities or bodies, taking account of their organisational structure and size.

4.  In cases other than those referred to in paragraph 1, the controller or processor or associations and other bodies representing categories of controllers or processors may or, where required by Union or Member State law shall, designate a data protection officer. The data protection officer may act for such associations and other bodies representing controllers or processors.

5.  The data protection officer shall be designated on the basis of professional qualities and, in particular, expert knowledge of data protection law and practices and the ability to fulfil the tasks referred to in Article 39.

6.  The data protection officer may be a staff member of the controller or processor, or fulfil the tasks on the basis of a service contract.

7.  The controller or the processor shall publish the contact details of the data protection officer and communicate them to the supervisory authority.

***

## CHAPTER V
*Transfers of personal data to third countries or international organisations*

Article 44. General principle for transfers

Any transfer of personal data which are undergoing processing or are intended for processing after transfer to a third country or to an international organisation shall take place only if, subject to the other provisions of this Regulation, the conditions laid down in this Chapter are complied with by the controller and processor, including for onward transfers of personal data from the third country or an international organisation to another third country or to another international organisation. All provisions in this Chapter shall be applied in order to ensure that the level of protection of natural persons guaranteed by this Regulation is not undermined.

Article 45. Transfers on the basis of an adequacy decision

1.  A transfer of personal data to a third country or an international organisation may take place where the Commission has decided that the third country, a territory or one or more specified sectors within that third country, or the international organisation in question ensures an adequate level of protection. Such a transfer shall not require any specific authorisation.

2.  When assessing the adequacy of the level of protection, the Commission shall, in particular, take account of the following elements:

(a) the rule of law, respect for human rights and fundamental freedoms, relevant legislation, both general and sectoral, including concerning public security, defence, national security and criminal law and the access of public authorities to personal data, as well as the implementation of such legislation, data protection rules, professional rules and security measures, including rules for the onward transfer of personal data to another third country or international organisation which are complied with in that country or international organisation, case-law, as well as effective and enforceable data subject rights and effective administrative and judicial redress for the data subjects whose personal data are being transferred;

(b) the existence and effective functioning of one or more independent supervisory authorities in the third country or to which an international organisation is subject, with responsibility for ensuring and enforcing compliance with the data protection rules, including adequate enforcement powers, for assisting and advising the data subjects in exercising their rights and for cooperation with the supervisory authorities of the Member States; and

(c) the international commitments the third country or international organisation concerned has entered into, or other obligations arising from legally binding conventions or instruments as well as from its participation in multilateral or regional systems, in particular in relation to the protection of personal data.

3.   The Commission, after assessing the adequacy of the level of protection, may decide, by means of implementing act, that a third country, a territory or one or more specified sectors within a third country, or an international organisation ensures an adequate level of protection within the meaning of paragraph 2 of this Article. The implementing act shall provide for a mechanism for a periodic review, at least every four years, which shall take into account all relevant developments in the third country or international organisation. The implementing act shall specify its territorial and sectoral application and, where applicable, identify the supervisory authority or authorities referred to in point (b) of paragraph 2 of this Article. The implementing act shall be adopted in accordance with the examination procedure referred to in Article 93(2).

4.   The Commission shall, on an ongoing basis, monitor developments in third countries and international organisations that could affect the functioning of decisions adopted pursuant to paragraph 3 of this Article and decisions adopted on the basis of Article 25(6) of Directive 95/46/EC.

5.   The Commission shall, where available information reveals, in particular following the review referred to in paragraph 3 of this Article, that a third country, a territory or one or more specified sectors within a third country, or an international organisation no longer ensures an adequate level of protection within the meaning of paragraph 2 of this Article, to the extent necessary, repeal, amend or suspend the decision referred to in paragraph 3 of this Article by means of implementing acts without retro-active effect. Those implementing acts shall be adopted in accordance with the examination procedure referred to in Article 93(2).

On duly justified imperative grounds of urgency, the Commission shall adopt immediately applicable implementing acts in accordance with the procedure referred to in Article 93(3).

6.  The Commission shall enter into consultations with the third country or international organisation with a view to remedying the situation giving rise to the decision made pursuant to paragraph 5.

7.  A decision pursuant to paragraph 5 of this Article is without prejudice to transfers of personal data to the third country, a territory or one or more specified sectors within that third country, or the international organisation in question pursuant to Articles 46 to 49.

8.  The Commission shall publish in the Official Journal of the European Union and on its website a list of the third countries, territories and specified sectors within a third country and international organisations for which it has decided that an adequate level of protection is or is no longer ensured.

9.  Decisions adopted by the Commission on the basis of Article 25(6) of Directive 95/46/EC shall remain in force until amended, replaced or repealed by a Commission Decision adopted in accordance with paragraph 3 or 5 of this Article.

Article 46. Transfers subject to appropriate safeguards

1.  In the absence of a decision pursuant to Article 45(3), a controller or processor may transfer personal data to a third country or an international organisation only if the controller or processor has provided appropriate safeguards, and on condition that enforceable data subject rights and effective legal remedies for data subjects are available.

2.  The appropriate safeguards referred to in paragraph 1 may be provided for, without requiring any specific authorisation from a supervisory authority, by:

>   (a) a legally binding and enforceable instrument between public authorities or bodies;

>   (b) binding corporate rules in accordance with Article 47;

>   (c) standard data protection clauses adopted by the Commission in accordance with the examination procedure referred to in Article 93(2);

>   (d) standard data protection clauses adopted by a supervisory authority and approved by the Commission pursuant to the examination procedure referred to in Article 93(2);

>   (e) an approved code of conduct pursuant to Article 40 together with binding and enforceable commitments of the controller or processor in the third country to apply the appropriate safeguards, including as regards data subjects' rights; or

>   (f) an approved certification mechanism pursuant to Article 42 together with binding and enforceable commitments of the controller or processor in the third country to apply the appropriate safeguards, including as regards data subjects' rights.

3.  Subject to the authorisation from the competent supervisory authority, the appropriate safeguards referred to in paragraph 1 may also be provided for, in particular, by:

>   (a) contractual clauses between the controller or processor and the controller, processor or the recipient of the personal data in the third country or international organisation; or

>   (b) provisions to be inserted into administrative arrangements between public authorities or bodies which include enforceable and effective data subject rights.

4.  The supervisory authority shall apply the consistency mechanism referred to in Article 63 in the cases referred to in paragraph 3 of this Article.

5.  Authorisations by a Member State or supervisory authority on the basis of Article 26(2) of Directive 95/46/EC shall remain valid until amended, replaced or repealed, if necessary, by that supervisory authority. Decisions adopted by the Commission on the basis of Article 26(4) of Directive 95/46/EC shall remain in force until amended, replaced or repealed, if necessary, by a Commission Decision adopted in accordance with paragraph 2 of this Article.

Article 47. Binding corporate rules

1.  The competent supervisory authority shall approve binding corporate rules in accordance with the consistency mechanism set out in Article 63, provided that they:

>   (a) are legally binding and apply to and are enforced by every member concerned of the group of undertakings, or group of enterprises engaged in a joint economic activity, including their employees;

>   (b) expressly confer enforceable rights on data subjects with regard to the processing of their personal data; and

>   (c) fulfil the requirements laid down in paragraph 2.

2.  The binding corporate rules referred to in paragraph 1 shall specify at least:

>   (a) the structure and contact details of the group of undertakings, or group of enterprises engaged in a joint economic activity and of each of its members;

>   (b) the data transfers or set of transfers, including the categories of personal data, the type of processing and its purposes, the type of data subjects affected and the identification of the third country or countries in question;

>   (c) their legally binding nature, both internally and externally;

(d) the application of the general data protection principles, in particular purpose limitation, data minimisation, limited storage periods, data quality, data protection by design and by default, legal basis for processing, processing of special categories of personal data, measures to ensure data security, and the requirements in respect of onward transfers to bodies not bound by the binding corporate rules;

(e) the rights of data subjects in regard to processing and the means to exercise those rights, including the right not to be subject to decisions based solely on automated processing, including profiling in accordance with Article 22, the right to lodge a complaint with the competent supervisory authority and before the competent courts of the Member States in accordance with Article 79, and to obtain redress and, where appropriate, compensation for a breach of the binding corporate rules;

(f) the acceptance by the controller or processor established on the territory of a Member State of liability for any breaches of the binding corporate rules by any member concerned not established in the Union; the controller or the processor shall be exempt from that liability, in whole or in part, only if it proves that that member is not responsible for the event giving rise to the damage;

(g) how the information on the binding corporate rules, in particular on the provisions referred to in points (d), (e) and (f) of this paragraph is provided to the data subjects in addition to Articles 13 and 14;

(h) the tasks of any data protection officer designated in accordance with Article 37 or any other person or entity in charge of the monitoring compliance with the binding corporate rules within the group of undertakings, or group of enterprises engaged in a joint economic activity, as well as monitoring training and complaint-handling;

(i) the complaint procedures;

(j) the mechanisms within the group of undertakings, or group of enterprises engaged in a joint economic activity for ensuring the verification of compliance with the binding corporate rules. Such mechanisms shall include data protection audits and methods for ensuring corrective actions to protect the rights of the data subject. Results of such verification should be communicated to the person or entity referred to in point (h) and to the board of the controlling undertaking of a group of undertakings, or of the group of enterprises engaged in a joint economic activity, and should be available upon request to the competent supervisory authority;

(k) the mechanisms for reporting and recording changes to the rules and reporting those changes to the supervisory authority;

(l) the cooperation mechanism with the supervisory authority to ensure compliance by any member of the group of undertakings, or group of enterprises engaged in a joint economic activity, in particular by making available to the supervisory authority the results of verifications of the measures referred to in point (j);

(m) the mechanisms for reporting to the competent supervisory authority any legal requirements to which a member of the group of undertakings, or group of enterprises engaged in a joint economic activity is subject in a third country which are likely to have a substantial adverse effect on the guarantees provided by the binding corporate rules; and

(n) the appropriate data protection training to personnel having permanent or regular access to personal data.

3.   The Commission may specify the format and procedures for the exchange of information between controllers, processors and supervisory authorities for binding corporate rules within the meaning of this Article. Those implementing acts shall be adopted in accordance with the examination procedure set out in Article 93(2). ***

Article 49. Derogations for specific situations

1.   In the absence of an adequacy decision pursuant to Article 45(3), or of appropriate safeguards pursuant to Article 46, including binding corporate rules, a transfer or a set of transfers of personal data to a third country or an international organisation shall take place only on one of the following conditions:

(a) the data subject has explicitly consented to the proposed transfer, after having been informed of the possible risks of such transfers for the data subject due to the absence of an adequacy decision and appropriate safeguards;

(b) the transfer is necessary for the performance of a contract between the data subject and the controller or the implementation of pre-contractual measures taken at the data subject's request;

(c) the transfer is necessary for the conclusion or performance of a contract concluded in the interest of the data subject between the controller and another natural or legal person;

(d) the transfer is necessary for important reasons of public interest;

(e) the transfer is necessary for the establishment, exercise or defence of legal claims;

(f) the transfer is necessary in order to protect the vital interests of the data subject or of other persons, where the data subject is physically or legally incapable of giving consent;

(g) the transfer is made from a register which according to Union or Member State law is intended to provide information to the public and which is open to consultation either by the public in general or by any person who can demonstrate a legitimate interest, but only to the extent that the conditions laid down by Union or Member State law for consultation are fulfilled in the particular case.

Where a transfer could not be based on a provision in Article 45 or 46, including the provisions on binding corporate rules, and none of the derogations for a specific situation referred to in the first subparagraph of this paragraph is applicable, a transfer to a third country or an international organisation may take place only if the transfer is not repetitive, concerns only a limited number of data subjects, is necessary for the purposes of compelling legitimate interests pursued by the controller which are not overridden by the interests or rights and freedoms of the data subject, and the controller has assessed all the circumstances surrounding the data transfer and has on the basis of that assessment provided suitable safeguards with regard to the protection of personal data. The controller shall inform the supervisory authority of the transfer. The controller shall, in addition to providing the information referred to in Articles 13 and 14, inform the data subject of the transfer and on the compelling legitimate interests pursued.

2. A transfer pursuant to point (g) of the first subparagraph of paragraph 1 shall not involve the entirety of the personal data or entire categories of the personal data contained in the register. Where the register is intended for consultation by persons having a legitimate interest, the transfer shall be made only at the request of those persons or if they are to be the recipients.

3. Points (a), (b) and (c) of the first subparagraph of paragraph 1 and the second subparagraph thereof shall not apply to activities carried out by public authorities in the exercise of their public powers.

4. The public interest referred to in point (d) of the first subparagraph of paragraph 1 shall be recognised in Union law or in the law of the Member State to which the controller is subject.

5. In the absence of an adequacy decision, Union or Member State law may, for important reasons of public interest, expressly set limits to the transfer of specific categories of personal data to a third country or an international organisation. Member States shall notify such provisions to the Commission.

6. The controller or processor shall document the assessment as well as the suitable safeguards referred to in the second subparagraph of paragraph 1 of this Article in the records referred to in Article 30.

Article 50. International cooperation for the protection of personal data

In relation to third countries and international organisations, the Commission and supervisory authorities shall take appropriate steps to:

> (a) develop international cooperation mechanisms to facilitate the effective enforcement of legislation for the protection of personal data;

> (b) provide international mutual assistance in the enforcement of legislation for the protection of personal data, including through notification, complaint referral, investigative assistance and information exchange, subject to appropriate safeguards for the protection of personal data and other fundamental rights and freedoms;

> (c) engage relevant stakeholders in discussion and activities aimed at furthering international cooperation in the enforcement of legislation for the protection of personal data;

(d) promote the exchange and documentation of personal data protection legislation and practice, including on jurisdictional conflicts with third countries.

\*\*\*

## CHAPTER VIII
### Remedies, liability and penalties

Article 77. Right to lodge a complaint with a supervisory authority

1. Without prejudice to any other administrative or judicial remedy, every data subject shall have the right to lodge a complaint with a supervisory authority, in particular in the Member State of his or her habitual residence, place of work or place of the alleged infringement if the data subject considers that the processing of personal data relating to him or her infringes this Regulation.

2. The supervisory authority with which the complaint has been lodged shall inform the complainant on the progress and the outcome of the complaint including the possibility of a judicial remedy pursuant to Article 78.

Article 78. Right to an effective judicial remedy against a supervisory authority

1. Without prejudice to any other administrative or non-judicial remedy, each natural or legal person shall have the right to an effective judicial remedy against a legally binding decision of a supervisory authority concerning them.

2. Without prejudice to any other administrative or non-judicial remedy, each data subject shall have the right to a an effective judicial remedy where the supervisory authority which is competent pursuant to Articles 55 and 56 does not handle a complaint or does not inform the data subject within three months on the progress or outcome of the complaint lodged pursuant to Article 77.

3. Proceedings against a supervisory authority shall be brought before the courts of the Member State where the supervisory authority is established.

4. Where proceedings are brought against a decision of a supervisory authority which was preceded by an opinion or a decision of the Board in the consistency mechanism, the supervisory authority shall forward that opinion or decision to the court.

Article 79. Right to an effective judicial remedy against a controller or processor

1. Without prejudice to any available administrative or non-judicial remedy, including the right to lodge a complaint with a supervisory authority pursuant to Article 77, each data subject shall have the right to an effective judicial remedy where he or she considers that his or her rights under this Regulation have been infringed as a result of the processing of his or her personal data in non-compliance with this Regulation.

2. Proceedings against a controller or a processor shall be brought before the courts of the Member State where the controller or processor has an establishment. Alternatively, such proceedings may be brought before the courts of the Member State where the data subject has his or her habitual residence, unless the controller or processor is a public authority of a Member State acting in the exercise of its public powers.

Article 80. Representation of data subjects

1. The data subject shall have the right to mandate a not-for-profit body, organisation or association which has been properly constituted in accordance with the law of a Member State, has statutory objectives which are in the public interest, and is active in the field of the protection of data subjects' rights and freedoms with regard to the protection of their personal data to lodge the complaint on his or her behalf, to exercise the rights referred to in Articles 77, 78 and 79 on his or her behalf, and to exercise the right to receive compensation referred to in Article 82 on his or her behalf where provided for by Member State law.

2. Member States may provide that any body, organisation or association referred to in paragraph 1 of this Article, independently of a data subject's mandate, has the right to lodge, in that Member State, a complaint with the supervisory authority which is competent pursuant to Article 77 and to exercise the rights referred to in Articles 78 and 79 if it considers that the rights of a data subject under this Regulation have been infringed as a result of the processing.

Article 81. Suspension of proceedings

1. Where a competent court of a Member State has information on proceedings, concerning the same subject matter as regards processing by the same controller or processor, that are pending in a court in another Member State, it shall contact that court in the other Member State to confirm the existence of such proceedings.

2. Where proceedings concerning the same subject matter as regards processing of the same controller or processor are pending in a court in another Member State, any competent court other than the court first seized may suspend its proceedings.

3. Where those proceedings are pending at first instance, any court other than the court first seized may also, on the application of one of the parties, decline jurisdiction if the court first seized has jurisdiction over the actions in question and its law permits the consolidation thereof.

Article 82. Right to compensation and liability

1. Any person who has suffered material or non-material damage as a result of an infringement of this Regulation shall have the right to receive compensation from the controller or processor for the damage suffered.

2. Any controller involved in processing shall be liable for the damage caused by processing which infringes this Regulation. A processor shall be liable for the damage caused by processing only where it has not complied with obligations of this Regulation specifically directed to processors or where it has acted outside or contrary to lawful instructions of the controller.

3. A controller or processor shall be exempt from liability under paragraph 2 if it proves that it is not in any way responsible for the event giving rise to the damage.

4. Where more than one controller or processor, or both a controller and a processor, are involved in the same processing and where they are, under paragraphs 2 and 3, responsible for any damage caused by processing, each controller or processor shall be held liable for the entire damage in order to ensure effective compensation of the data subject.

5. Where a controller or processor has, in accordance with paragraph 4, paid full compensation for the damage suffered, that controller or processor shall be entitled to claim back from the other controllers or processors involved in the same processing that part of the compensation corresponding to their part of responsibility for the damage, in accordance with the conditions set out in paragraph 2.

6. Court proceedings for exercising the right to receive compensation shall be brought before the courts competent under the law of the Member State referred to in Article 79(2).

Article 83. General conditions for imposing administrative fines

1. Each supervisory authority shall ensure that the imposition of administrative fines pursuant to this Article in respect of infringements of this Regulation referred to in paragraphs 4, 5 and 6 shall in each individual case be effective, proportionate and dissuasive.

2. Administrative fines shall, depending on the circumstances of each individual case, be imposed in addition to, or instead of, measures referred to in points (a) to (h) and (j) of Article 58(2). When deciding whether to impose an administrative fine and deciding on the amount of the administrative fine in each individual case due regard shall be given to the following:

(a) the nature, gravity and duration of the infringement taking into account the nature scope or purpose of the processing concerned as well as the number of data subjects affected and the level of damage suffered by them;

(b) the intentional or negligent character of the infringement;

(c) any action taken by the controller or processor to mitigate the damage suffered by data subjects;

(d) the degree of responsibility of the controller or processor taking into account technical and organisational measures implemented by them pursuant to Articles 25 and 32;

(e) any relevant previous infringements by the controller or processor;

(f) the degree of cooperation with the supervisory authority, in order to remedy the infringement and mitigate the possible adverse effects of the infringement;

(g) the categories of personal data affected by the infringement;

(h) the manner in which the infringement became known to the supervisory authority, in particular whether, and if so to what extent, the controller or processor notified the infringement;

(i) where measures referred to in Article 58(2) have previously been ordered against the controller or processor concerned with regard to the same subject-matter, compliance with those measures;

(j) adherence to approved codes of conduct pursuant to Article 40 or approved certification mechanisms pursuant to Article 42; and

(k) any other aggravating or mitigating factor applicable to the circumstances of the case, such as financial benefits gained, or losses avoided, directly or indirectly, from the infringement.

3.  If a controller or processor intentionally or negligently, for the same or linked processing operations, infringes several provisions of this Regulation, the total amount of the administrative fine shall not exceed the amount specified for the gravest infringement.

4.  Infringements of the following provisions shall, in accordance with paragraph 2, be subject to administrative fines up to 10 000 000 EUR, or in the case of an undertaking, up to 2 % of the total worldwide annual turnover of the preceding financial year, whichever is higher:

(a) the obligations of the controller and the processor pursuant to Articles 8, 11, 25 to 39 and 42 and 43;

(b) the obligations of the certification body pursuant to Articles 42 and 43;

(c) the obligations of the monitoring body pursuant to Article 41(4).

5.  Infringements of the following provisions shall, in accordance with paragraph 2, be subject to administrative fines up to 20 000 000 EUR, or in the case of an undertaking, up to 4 % of the total worldwide annual turnover of the preceding financial year, whichever is higher:

(a) the basic principles for processing, including conditions for consent, pursuant to Articles 5, 6, 7 and 9;

(b) the data subjects' rights pursuant to Articles 12 to 22;

(c) the transfers of personal data to a recipient in a third country or an international organisation pursuant to Articles 44 to 49;

(d) any obligations pursuant to Member State law adopted under Chapter IX;

(e) non-compliance with an order or a temporary or definitive limitation on processing or the suspension of data flows by the supervisory authority pursuant to Article 58(2) or failure to provide access in violation of Article 58(1).

6.  Non-compliance with an order by the supervisory authority as referred to in Article 58(2) shall, in accordance with paragraph 2 of this Article, be subject to administrative fines up to 20 000 000 EUR, or in the case of an undertaking, up to 4 % of the total worldwide annual turnover of the preceding financial year, whichever is higher.

7.  Without prejudice to the corrective powers of supervisory authorities pursuant to Article 58(2), each Member State may lay down the rules on whether and to what extent administrative fines may be imposed on public authorities and bodies established in that Member State.

8.  The exercise by the supervisory authority of its powers under this Article shall be subject to appropriate procedural safeguards in accordance with Union and Member State law, including effective judicial remedy and due process.

9.  Where the legal system of the Member State does not provide for administrative fines, this Article may be applied in such a manner that the fine is initiated by the competent supervisory authority and imposed by competent national courts, while ensuring that those legal remedies are effective and have an equivalent effect to the administrative fines imposed by supervisory authorities. In any event, the fines imposed shall be effective, proportionate and dissuasive. Those Member States shall notify to the Commission the provisions of their laws which they adopt pursuant to this paragraph by 25 May 2018 and, without delay, any subsequent amendment law or amendment affecting them.

Article 84. Penalties

1.  Member States shall lay down the rules on other penalties applicable to infringements of this Regulation in particular for infringements which are not subject to administrative fines pursuant to Article 83, and shall take all measures necessary to ensure that they are implemented. Such penalties shall be effective, proportionate and dissuasive.

2.  Each Member State shall notify to the Commission the provisions of its law which it adopts pursuant to paragraph 1, by 25 May 2018 and, without delay, any subsequent amendment affecting them.

## CHAPTER IX
### Provisions relating to specific processing situations

Article 85. Processing and freedom of expression and information

1.  Member States shall by law reconcile the right to the protection of personal data pursuant to this Regulation with the right to freedom of expression and information, including processing for journalistic purposes and the purposes of academic, artistic or literary expression.

2.  For processing carried out for journalistic purposes or the purpose of academic artistic or literary expression, Member States shall provide for exemptions or derogations from Chapter II (principles), Chapter III (rights of the data subject), Chapter IV (controller and processor), Chapter V (transfer of personal data to third countries or international organisations), Chapter VI (independent supervisory authorities), Chapter VII (cooperation and consistency) and Chapter IX (specific data processing situations) if they are necessary to reconcile the right to the protection of personal data with the freedom of expression and information.

# CHILDREN'S ONLINE PRIVACY PROTECTION ACT OF 1998 (COPPA)
## *15 U.S.C. §§ 6501–6506*
### (enacted October 21, 1998)

15 U.S. Code § 6501 - Definitions

In this chapter:

(1) Child. The term "child" means an individual under the age of 13.

(2) Operator The term "operator"—

(A) means any person who operates a website located on the Internet or an online service and who collects or maintains personal information from or about the users of or visitors to such website or online service, or on whose behalf such information is collected or maintained, where such website or online service is operated for commercial purposes, including any person offering products or services for sale through that website or online service, involving commerce—

(i) among the several States or with 1 or more foreign nations;

(ii) in any territory of the United States or in the District of Columbia, or between any such territory and—

(I) another such territory; or

(II) any State or foreign nation; or

(iii) between the District of Columbia and any State, territory, or foreign nation; but

(B) does not include any nonprofit entity that would otherwise be exempt from coverage under section 45 of this title.

(3) Commission. The term "Commission" means the Federal Trade Commission.

(4) Disclosure. The term "disclosure" means, with respect to personal information—

(A) the release of personal information collected from a child in identifiable form by an operator for any purpose, except where such information is provided to a person other than the operator who provides support for the internal operations of the website and does not disclose or use that information for any other purpose; and

(B) making personal information collected from a child by a website or online service directed to children or with actual knowledge that such information was collected from a child, publicly available in identifiable form, by any means including by a public posting, through the Internet, or through—

(i) a home page of a website;

(ii) a pen pal service;

(iii) an electronic mail service;

(iv) a message board; or

(v) a chat room.

(5) Federal agency. The term "Federal agency" means an agency, as that term is defined in section 551(1) of title 5.

(6) Internet. The term "Internet" means collectively the myriad of computer and telecommunications facilities, including equipment and operating software, which comprise the interconnected world-wide network of networks that employ the Transmission Control Protocol/Internet Protocol, or any predecessor or successor protocols to such protocol, to communicate information of all kinds by wire or radio.

(7) Parent. The term "parent" includes a legal guardian.

(8) Personal information. The term "personal information" means individually identifiable information about an individual collected online, including—

(A) a first and last name;

(B) a home or other physical address including street name and name of a city or town;

(C) an e-mail address;

(D) a telephone number;

(E) a Social Security number;

(F) any other identifier that the Commission determines permits the physical or online contacting of a specific individual; or

(G) information concerning the child or the parents of that child that the website collects online from the child and combines with an identifier described in this paragraph.

(9) Verifiable parental consent. The term "verifiable parental consent" means any reasonable effort (taking into consideration available technology), including a request for authorization for future collection, use, and disclosure described in the notice, to ensure that a parent of a child receives notice of the operator's personal information collection, use, and disclosure practices, and authorizes the collection, use, and disclosure, as applicable, of personal information and the subsequent use of that information before that information is collected from that child.

(10) Website or online service directed to children

(A) In general. The term "website or online service directed to children" means—

(i) a commercial website or online service that is targeted to children; or

(ii) that portion of a commercial website or online service that is targeted to children.

(B) Limitation

A commercial website or online service, or a portion of a commercial website or online service, shall not be deemed directed to children solely for referring or linking to a commercial website or online service directed to children by using information location tools, including a directory, index, reference, pointer, or hypertext link.

(11) Person. The term "person" means any individual, partnership, corporation, trust, estate, cooperative, association, or other entity.

(12) Online contact information. The term "online contact information" means an e-mail address or another substantially similar identifier that permits direct contact with a person online.

15 U.S. Code § 6502 – Regulation of Unfair and Deceptive Acts and Practices in Connection with Collection and Use of Personal Information from and About Children on the Internet

(a) Acts prohibited

(1) In general. It is unlawful for an operator of a website or online service directed to children, or any operator that has actual knowledge that it is collecting personal information from a child, to collect personal information from a child in a manner that violates the regulations prescribed under subsection (b).

(2) Disclosure to parent protected. Notwithstanding paragraph (1), neither an operator of such a website or online service nor the operator's agent shall be held to be liable under any Federal or State law for any disclosure made in good faith and following reasonable procedures in responding to a request for disclosure of personal information under subsection (b)(1)(B)(iii) to the parent of a child.

(b) Regulations

(1) In general. Not later than 1 year after October 21, 1998, the Commission shall promulgate under section 553 of title 5 regulations that—

(A) require the operator of any website or online service directed to children that collects personal information from children or the operator of a website or online service that has actual knowledge that it is collecting personal information from a child—

(i) to provide notice on the website of what information is collected from children by the operator, how the operator uses such information, and the operator's disclosure practices for such information; and

(ii) to obtain verifiable parental consent for the collection, use, or disclosure of personal information from children;

(B) require the operator to provide, upon request of a parent under this subparagraph whose child has provided personal information to that website or online service, upon proper identification of that parent, to such parent—

(i) a description of the specific types of personal information collected from the child by that operator;

(ii) the opportunity at any time to refuse to permit the operator's further use or maintenance in retrievable form, or future online collection, of personal information from that child; and

(iii) notwithstanding any other provision of law, a means that is reasonable under the circumstances for the parent to obtain any personal information collected from that child;

(C) prohibit conditioning a child's participation in a game, the offering of a prize, or another activity on the child disclosing more personal information than is reasonably necessary to participate in such activity; and

(D) require the operator of such a website or online service to establish and maintain reasonable procedures to protect the confidentiality, security, and integrity of personal information collected from children.

(2) When consent not required. The regulations shall provide that verifiable parental consent under paragraph (1)(A)(ii) is not required in the case of—

(A) online contact information collected from a child that is used only to respond directly on a one-time basis to a specific request from the child and is not used to recontact the child and is not maintained in retrievable form by the operator;

(B) a request for the name or online contact information of a parent or child that is used for the sole purpose of obtaining parental consent or providing notice under this section and where such information is not maintained in retrievable form by the operator if parental consent is not obtained after a reasonable time;

(C)online contact information collected from a child that is used only to respond more than once directly to a specific request from the child and is not used to recontact the child beyond the scope of that request—

(i) if, before any additional response after the initial response to the child, the operator uses reasonable efforts to provide a parent notice of the online contact information collected from the child, the purposes for which it is to be used, and an opportunity for the parent to request that the operator make no further use of the information and that it not be maintained in retrievable form; or

(ii) without notice to the parent in such circumstances as the Commission may determine are appropriate, taking into consideration the benefits to the child of access to information and services, and risks to the security and privacy of the child, in regulations promulgated under this subsection;

(D) the name of the child and online contact information (to the extent reasonably necessary to protect the safety of a child participant on the site)—

(i) used only for the purpose of protecting such safety;

(ii) not used to recontact the child or for any other purpose; and

(iii) not disclosed on the site,

if the operator uses reasonable efforts to provide a parent notice of the name and online contact information collected from the child, the purposes for which it is to be used, and an opportunity for the parent to request that the operator make no further use of the information and that it not be maintained in retrievable form; or

(E) the collection, use, or dissemination of such information by the operator of such a website or online service necessary—

> (i) to protect the security or integrity of its website;
>
> (ii) to take precautions against liability;
>
> (iii) to respond to judicial process; or
>
> (iv) to the extent permitted under other provisions of law, to provide information to law enforcement agencies or for an investigation on a matter related to public safety.

(3) Termination of service. The regulations shall permit the operator of a website or an online service to terminate service provided to a child whose parent has refused, under the regulations prescribed under paragraph (1)(B)(ii), to permit the operator's further use or maintenance in retrievable form, or future online collection, of personal information from that child.

(c) Enforcement. Subject to sections 6503 and 6505 of this title, a violation of a regulation prescribed under subsection (a) shall be treated as a violation of a rule defining an unfair or deceptive act or practice prescribed under section 57a(a)(1)(B) of this title.

(d) Inconsistent State law. No State or local government may impose any liability for commercial activities or actions by operators in interstate or foreign commerce in connection with an activity or action described in this chapter that is inconsistent with the treatment of those activities or actions under this section.

15 U.S. Code § 6503 – Safe Harbors

(a) Guidelines. An operator may satisfy the requirements of regulations issued under section 6502(b) of this title by following a set of self-regulatory guidelines, issued by representatives of the marketing or online industries, or by other persons, approved under subsection (b).

(b) Incentives

(1) Self-regulatory incentives. In prescribing regulations under section 6502 of this title, the Commission shall provide incentives for self-regulation by operators to implement the protections afforded children under the regulatory requirements described in subsection (b) of that section.

(2) Deemed compliance. Such incentives shall include provisions for ensuring that a person will be deemed to be in compliance with the requirements of the regulations under section 6502 of this title if that person complies with guidelines that, after notice and comment, are approved by the Commission upon making a determination that the guidelines meet the requirements of the regulations issued under section 6502 of this title.

(3) Expedited response to requests. The Commission shall act upon requests for safe harbor treatment within 180 days of the filing of the request, and shall set forth in writing its conclusions with regard to such requests.

(c) Appeals. Final action by the Commission on a request for approval of guidelines, or the failure to act within 180 days on a request for approval of guidelines, submitted under subsection (b) may be appealed to a district court of the United States of appropriate jurisdiction as provided for in section 706 of title 5.

15 U.S. Code § 6504 – Actions by States

(a) In general

> (1) Civil actions. In any case in which the attorney general of a State has reason to believe that an interest of the residents of that State has been or is threatened or adversely affected by the engagement of any person in a practice that violates any regulation of the Commission prescribed under section 6502(b) of this title, the State, as *parens patriae*, may bring a civil action on behalf of the residents of the State in a district court of the United States of appropriate jurisdiction to—

>> (A) enjoin that practice;

>> (B) enforce compliance with the regulation;

>> (C) obtain damage, restitution, or other compensation on behalf of residents of the State; or

>> (D) obtain such other relief as the court may consider to be appropriate.

> (2) Notice

>> (A) In general. Before filing an action under paragraph (1), the attorney general of the State involved shall provide to the Commission—

>>> (i) written notice of that action; and

>>> (ii) a copy of the complaint for that action.

>> (B) Exemption

>>> (i) In general. Subparagraph (A) shall not apply with respect to the filing of an action by an attorney general of a State under this subsection, if the attorney general determines that it is not feasible to provide the notice described in that subparagraph before the filing of the action.

>>> (ii) Notification. In an action described in clause (i), the attorney general of a State shall provide notice and a copy of the complaint to the Commission at the same time as the attorney general files the action.

(b) Intervention

> (1) In general. On receiving notice under subsection (a)(2), the Commission shall have the right to intervene in the action that is the subject of the notice.

> (2) Effect of intervention. If the Commission intervenes in an action under subsection (a), it shall have the right—

>> (A) to be heard with respect to any matter that arises in that action; and

>> (B) to file a petition for appeal.

(3) Amicus curiae. Upon application to the court, a person whose self-regulatory guidelines have been approved by the Commission and are relied upon as a defense by any defendant to a proceeding under this section may file amicus curiae in that proceeding.

(c) Construction. For purposes of bringing any civil action under subsection (a), nothing in this chapter shall be construed to prevent an attorney general of a State from exercising the powers conferred on the attorney general by the laws of that State to—

(1) conduct investigations;

(2) administer oaths or affirmations; or

(3) compel the attendance of witnesses or the production of documentary and other evidence.

(d) Actions by Commission. In any case in which an action is instituted by or on behalf of the Commission for violation of any regulation prescribed under section 6502 of this title, no State may, during the pendency of that action, institute an action under subsection (a) against any defendant named in the complaint in that action for violation of that regulation.

(e) Venue; service of process

(1) Venue. Any action brought under subsection (a) may be brought in the district court of the United States that meets applicable requirements relating to venue under section 1391 of title 28.

(2) Service of process. In an action brought under subsection (a), process may be served in any district in which the defendant—

(A) is an inhabitant; or

(B) may be found.

15 U.S. Code § 6505 – Administration and Applicability

(a) In general. Except as otherwise provided, this chapter shall be enforced by the Commission under the Federal Trade Commission Act (15 U.S.C. 41 et seq.).

(b) Provisions. Compliance with the requirements imposed under this chapter shall be enforced under—

(1) section 8 of the Federal Deposit Insurance Act (12 U.S.C. 1818), in the case of—

(A) national banks, and Federal branches and Federal agencies of foreign banks, by the Office of the Comptroller of the Currency;

(B) member banks of the Federal Reserve System (other than national banks), branches and agencies of foreign banks (other than Federal branches, Federal agencies, and insured State branches of foreign banks), commercial lending companies owned or controlled by foreign banks, and organizations operating under section 25 or 25(a) [1] of the Federal Reserve Act (12 U.S.C. 601 et seq. and 611 et. seq.), by the Board; and

(C) banks insured by the Federal Deposit Insurance Corporation (other than members of the Federal Reserve System) and insured State branches of foreign banks, by the Board of Directors of the Federal Deposit Insurance Corporation;

(2) section 8 of the Federal Deposit Insurance Act (12 U.S.C. 1818), by the Director of the Office of Thrift Supervision, in the case of a savings association the deposits of which are insured by the Federal Deposit Insurance Corporation;

(3) the Federal Credit Union Act (12 U.S.C. 1751 et seq.) by the National Credit Union Administration Board with respect to any Federal credit union;

(4) part A of subtitle VII of title 49 by the Secretary of Transportation with respect to any air carrier or foreign air carrier subject to that part;

(5) the Packers and Stockyards Act, 1921 (7 U.S.C. 181 et. seq.) (except as provided in section 406 of that Act (7 U.S.C. 226, 227)), by the Secretary of Agriculture with respect to any activities subject to that Act; and

(6) the Farm Credit Act of 1971 (12 U.S.C. 2001 et seq.) by the Farm Credit Administration with respect to any Federal land bank, Federal land bank association, Federal intermediate credit bank, or production credit association.

(c) Exercise of certain powers. For the purpose of the exercise by any agency referred to in subsection (a) [2] of its powers under any Act referred to in that subsection, a violation of any requirement imposed under this chapter shall be deemed to be a violation of a requirement imposed under that Act. In addition to its powers under any provision of law specifically referred to in subsection (a),[2] each of the agencies referred to in that subsection may exercise, for the purpose of enforcing compliance with any requirement imposed under this chapter, any other authority conferred on it by law.

(d) Actions by Commission. The Commission shall prevent any person from violating a rule of the Commission under section 6502 of this title in the same manner, by the same means, and with the same jurisdiction, powers, and duties as though all applicable terms and provisions of the Federal Trade Commission Act (15 U.S.C. 41 et seq.) were incorporated into and made a part of this chapter. Any entity that violates such rule shall be subject to the penalties and entitled to the privileges and immunities provided in the Federal Trade Commission Act in the same manner, by the same means, and with the same jurisdiction, power, and duties as though all applicable terms and provisions of the Federal Trade Commission Act were incorporated into and made a part of this chapter.

(e) Effect on other laws. Nothing contained in this chapter shall be construed to limit the authority of the Commission under any other provisions of law.

15 U.S. Code § 6506 - Review

Not later than 5 years after the effective date of the regulations initially issued under section 6502 of this title, the Commission shall—

(1) review the implementation of this chapter, including the effect of the implementation of this chapter on practices relating to the collection and disclosure of information relating to children, children's ability to obtain access to information of their choice online, and on the availability of websites directed to children; and

(2) prepare and submit to Congress a report on the results of the review under paragraph (1)

# California Data Breach Notification Law (2003)
## Cal. Civ. Code § 1798.82 (2003)

§ 1798.82. Disclosure of breach of security by business that owns or maintains computerized data

(a) Any person or business that conducts business in California, and that owns or licenses computerized data that includes personal information, shall disclose any breach of the security of the system following discovery or notification of the breach in the security of the data to any resident of California whose unencrypted personal information was, or is reasonably believed to have been, acquired by an unauthorized person. The disclosure shall be made in the most expedient time possible and without unreasonable delay, consistent with the legitimate needs of law enforcement, as provided in subdivision (c), or any measures necessary to determine the scope of the breach and restore the reasonable integrity of the data system.

(b) Any person or business that maintains computerized data that includes personal information that the person or business does not own shall notify the owner or licensee of the information of any breach of the security of the data immediately following discovery, if the personal information was, or is reasonably believed to have been, acquired by an unauthorized person.

(c) The notification required by this section may be delayed if a law enforcement agency determines that the notification will impede a criminal investigation. The notification required by this section shall be made after the law enforcement agency determines that it will not compromise the investigation.

(d) For purposes of this section, "breach of the security of the system" means unauthorized acquisition of computerized data that compromises the security, confidentiality, or integrity of personal information maintained by the person or business. Good faith acquisition of personal information by an employee or agent of the person or business for the purposes of the person or business is not a breach of the security of the system, provided that the personal information is not used or subject to further unauthorized disclosure.

(e) For purposes of this section, "personal information" means an individual's first name or first initial and last name in combination with any one or more of the following data elements, when either the name or the data elements are not encrypted:

(1) Social security number.

(2) Driver's license number or California Identification Card number.

(3) Account number, credit or debit card number, in combination with any required security code, access code, or password that would permit access to an individual's financial account.

(4) Medical information.

(5) Health insurance information.

(f)    (1) For purposes of this section, "personal information" does not include publicly available information that is lawfully made available to the general public from federal, state, or local government records.

(2) For purposes of this section, "medical information" means any information regarding an individual's medical history, mental or physical condition, or medical treatment or diagnosis by a health care professional.

(3) For purposes of this section, "health insurance information" means an individual's health insurance policy number or subscriber identification number, any unique identifier used by a health insurer to identify the individual, or any information in an individual's application and claims history, including any appeals records.

(g) For purposes of this section, "notice" may be provided by one of the following methods:

(1) Written notice.

(2) Electronic notice, if the notice provided is consistent with the provisions regarding electronic records and signatures set forth in Section 7001 of Title 15 of the United States Code.

(3) Substitute notice, if the person or business demonstrates that the cost of providing notice would exceed two hundred fifty thousand dollars ($250,000), or that the affected class of subject persons to be notified exceeds 500,000, or the person or business does not have sufficient contact information. Substitute notice shall consist of all of the following:

(A) E-mail notice when the person or business has an e-mail address for the subject persons.

(B) Conspicuous posting of the notice on the Web site page of the person or business, if the person or business maintains one.

(C) Notification to major statewide media.

(h) Notwithstanding subdivision (g), a person or business that maintains its own notification procedures as part of an information security policy for the treatment of personal information and is otherwise consistent with the timing requirements of this part, shall be deemed to be in compliance with the notification requirements of this section if the person or business notifies subject persons in accordance with its policies in the event of a breach of security of the system.

# CALIFORNIA ONLINE PRIVACY PROTECTION ACT (2003)
### Cal. Bus. & Prof. Code § 22575 - 22577 (2003)

### § 22575. Posting or availability of privacy policy;

(a) An operator of a commercial Web site or online service that collects personally identifiable information through the Internet about individual consumers residing in California who use or visit its commercial Web site or online service shall conspicuously post its privacy policy on its Web site, or in the case of an operator of an online service, make that policy available in accordance with paragraph (5) of subdivision (b) of Section 22577. An operator shall be in violation of this subdivision only if the operator fails to post its policy within 30 days after being notified of noncompliance.

(b) The privacy policy required by subdivision (a) shall do all of the following:

(1) Identify the categories of personally identifiable information that the operator collects through the Web site or online service about individual consumers who use or visit its commercial Web site or online service and the categories of third-party persons or entities with whom the operator may share that personally identifiable information.

(2) If the operator maintains a process for an individual consumer who uses or visits its commercial Web site or online service to review and request changes to any of his or her personally identifiable information that is collected through the Web site or online service, provide a description of that process.

(3) Describe the process by which the operator notifies consumers who use or visit its commercial Web site or online service of material changes to the operator's privacy policy for that Web site or online service.

(4) Identify its effective date.

### § 22576. Violations.

An operator of a commercial Web site or online service that collects personally identifiable information through the Web site or online service from individual consumers who use or visit the commercial Web site or online service and who reside in California shall be in violation of this section if the operator fails to comply with the provisions of Section 22575 or with the provisions of its posted privacy policy in either of the following ways:

(a) Knowingly and willfully.

(b) Negligently and materially.

### § 22577. Definitions

For the purposes of this chapter, the following definitions apply:

(a) The term "personally identifiable information" means individually identifiable information about an individual consumer collected online by the operator from that individual and maintained by the operator in an accessible form, including any of the following:

(1) A first and last name.

(2) A home or other physical address, including street name and name of a city or town.

(3) An e-mail address.

(4) A telephone number.

(5) A social security number.

(6) Any other identifier that permits the physical or online contacting of a specific individual.

(7) Information concerning a user that the Web site or online service collects online from the user and maintains in personally identifiable form in combination with an identifier described in this subdivision.

(b) The term "conspicuously post" with respect to a privacy policy shall include posting the privacy policy through any of the following:

(1) A Web page on which the actual privacy policy is posted if the Web page is the homepage or first significant page after entering the Web site.

(2) An icon that hyperlinks to a Web page on which the actual privacy policy is posted, if the icon is located on the homepage or the first significant page after entering the Web site, and if the icon contains the word "privacy." The icon shall also use a color that contrasts with the background color of the Web page or is otherwise distinguishable.

(3) A text link that hyperlinks to a Web page on which the actual privacy policy is posted, if the text link is located on the homepage or first significant page after entering the Web site, and if the text link does one of the following:

(A) Includes the word "privacy."

(B) Is written in capital letters equal to or greater in size than the surrounding text.

(C) Is written in larger type than the surrounding text, or in contrasting type, font, or color to the surrounding text of the same size, or set off from the surrounding text of the same size by symbols or other marks that call attention to the language.

(4) Any other functional hyperlink that is so displayed that a reasonable person would notice it.

(5) In the case of an online service, any other reasonably accessible means of making the privacy policy available for consumers of the online service.

(c) The term "operator" means any person or entity that owns a Web site located on the Internet or an online service that collects and maintains personally identifiable information from a consumer residing in California who uses or visits the Web site or online service if the Web site or online service is operated for commercial purposes. It does not include any third party that operates, hosts, or manages, but does not own, a Web site or online service on the owner's behalf or by processing information on behalf of the owner.

(d) The term "consumer" means any individual who seeks or acquires, by purchase or lease, any goods, services, money, or credit for personal, family, or household purposes.

# CALIFORNIA CONSUMER PRIVACY ACT (CCPA) (2018)
## Cal. Civil Code § 1798.100, et seq.

*Editor's Note: In November 2020, California voters approved the California Privacy Rights Act (CPRA), which significantly modifies the CCPA. The CPRA establishes a new California Privacy Rights Agency, which is tasked with issuing regulations as well as enforcement. Most of CPRA's substantive provisions become effective January 1, 2023.*

*In 2021, Colorado and Virginia also passed broad consumer privacy statutes.*

***

Section 1798.100.

(a) A consumer shall have the right to request that a business that collects a consumer's personal information disclose to that consumer the categories and specific pieces of personal information the business has collected.

(b) A business that collects a consumer's personal information shall, at or before the point of collection, inform consumers as to the categories of personal information to be collected and the purposes for which the categories of personal information shall be used. A business shall not collect additional categories of personal information or use personal information collected for additional purposes without providing the consumer with notice consistent with this section.

(c) A business shall provide the information specified in subdivision (a) to a consumer only upon receipt of a verifiable consumer request.

(d) A business that receives a verifiable consumer request from a consumer to access personal information shall promptly take steps to disclose and deliver, free of charge to the consumer, the personal information required by this section. The information may be delivered by mail or electronically, and if provided electronically, the information shall be in a portable and, to the extent technically feasible, in a readily useable format that allows the consumer to transmit this information to another entity without hindrance. A business may provide personal information to a consumer at any time, but shall not be required to provide personal information to a consumer more than twice in a 12-month period.

(e) This section shall not require a business to retain any personal information collected for a single, one-time transaction, if such information is not sold or retained by the business or to reidentify or otherwise link information that is not maintained in a manner that would be considered personal information.

> (1) Retain any personal information collected for a single, one-time transaction, if the information is not sold or retained by the business.

> (2) Reidentify or otherwise link any data that, in the ordinary course of business, is not maintained in a manner that would be considered personal information.

Section 1798.105.

(a) A consumer shall have the right to request that a business delete any personal information about the consumer which the business has collected from the consumer.

(b) A business that collects personal information about consumers shall disclose, pursuant to subparagraph (A) of paragraph (5) of subdivision (a) of Section 1798.130, the consumer's rights to request the deletion of the consumer's personal information.

(c) A business that receives a verifiable request from a consumer to delete the consumer's personal information pursuant to subdivision (a) of this section shall delete the consumer's personal information from its records and direct any service providers to delete the consumer's personal information from their records.

(d) A business or a service provider shall not be required to comply with a consumer's request to delete the consumer's personal information if it is necessary for the business or service provider to maintain the consumer's personal information in order to:

> (1) Complete the transaction for which the personal information was collected, provide a good or service requested by the consumer, or reasonably anticipated within the context of a business's ongoing business relationship with the consumer, or otherwise perform a contract between the business and the consumer.

> (2) Detect security incidents, protect against malicious, deceptive, fraudulent, or illegal activity; or prosecute those responsible for that activity.

> (3) Debug to identify and repair errors that impair existing intended functionality.

> (4) Exercise free speech, ensure the right of another consumer to exercise his or her right of free speech, or exercise another right provided for by law.

> (5) Comply with the California Electronic Communications Privacy Act pursuant to Chapter 3.6 (commencing with Section 1546) of Title 12 of Part 2 of the Penal Code.

> (6) Engage in public or peer-reviewed scientific, historical, or statistical research in the public interest that adheres to all other applicable ethics and privacy laws, when the businesses' deletion of the information is likely to render impossible or seriously impair the achievement of such research, if the consumer has provided informed consent.

> (7) To enable solely internal uses that are reasonably aligned with the expectations of the consumer based on the consumer's relationship with the business.

> (8) Comply with a legal obligation.

> (9) Otherwise use the consumer's personal information, internally, in a lawful manner that is compatible with the context in which the consumer provided the information.

Section 1798.110.

(a) A consumer shall have the right to request that a business that collects personal information about the consumer disclose to the consumer the following:

(1) The categories of personal information it has collected about that consumer.

(2) The categories of sources from which the personal information is collected.

(3) The business or commercial purpose for collecting or selling personal information.

(4) The categories of third parties with whom the business shares personal information.

(5) The specific pieces of personal information it has collected about that consumer.

(b) A business that collects personal information about a consumer shall disclose to the consumer, pursuant to paragraph (3) of subdivision (a) of Section 1798.130, the information specified in subdivision (a) upon receipt of a verifiable request from the consumer.

(c) A business that collects personal information about consumers shall disclose, pursuant to subparagraph (B) of paragraph (5) of subdivision (a) of Section 1798.130:

(1) The categories of personal information it has collected about that consumer.

(2) The categories of sources from which the personal information is collected.

(3) The business or commercial purpose for collecting or selling personal information.

(4) The categories of third parties with whom the business shares personal information.

(5) The specific pieces of personal information the business has collected about that consumer.

(d) This section does not require a business to do the following:

(1) Retain any personal information about a consumer collected for a single one-time transaction if, in the ordinary course of business, that information about the consumer is not retained.

(2) Reidentify or otherwise link any data that, in the ordinary course of business, is not maintained in a manner that would be considered personal information.

Section 1798.115.

(a) A consumer shall have the right to request that a business that sells the consumer's personal information, or that discloses it for a business purpose, disclose to that consumer:

(1) The categories of personal information that the business collected about the consumer.

(2) The categories of personal information that the business sold about the consumer and the categories of third parties to whom the personal information was sold, by category or categories of personal information for each third party to whom the personal information was sold.

(3) The categories of personal information that the business disclosed about the consumer for a business purpose.

(b) A business that sells personal information about a consumer, or that discloses a consumer's personal information for a business purpose, shall disclose, pursuant to paragraph (4) of subdivision (a) of Section

1798.130, the information specified in subdivision (a) to the consumer upon receipt of a verifiable request from the consumer.

(c) A business that sells consumers' personal information, or that discloses consumers' personal information for a business purpose, shall disclose, pursuant to subparagraph (C) of paragraph (5) of subdivision (a) of Section 1798.130:

> (1) The category or categories of consumers' personal information it has sold, or if the business has not sold consumers' personal information, it shall disclose that fact.

> (2) The category or categories of consumers' personal information it has disclosed for a business purpose, or if the business has not disclosed the consumers' personal information for a business purpose, it shall disclose that fact.

(d) A third party shall not sell personal information about a consumer that has been sold to the third party by a business unless the consumer has received explicit notice and is provided an opportunity to exercise the right to opt out pursuant to 1798.120.

Section 1798.120.

(a) A consumer shall have the right, at any time, to direct a business that sells personal information about the consumer to third parties not to sell the consumer's personal information. This right may be referred to as the right to opt out.

(b) A business that sells consumers' personal information to third parties shall provide notice to consumers, pursuant to subdivision (a) of Section 1798.135, that this information may be sold and that consumers have the right to opt out of the sale of their personal information.

(c) A business that has received direction from a consumer not to sell the consumer's personal information or, in the case of a minor consumer's personal information has not received consent to sell the minor consumer's personal information shall be prohibited, pursuant to paragraph (4) of subdivision (a) of Section 1798.135, from selling the consumer's personal information after its receipt of the consumer's direction, unless the consumer subsequently provides express authorization for the sale of the consumer's personal information.

(d) Notwithstanding subdivision (a), a business shall not sell the personal information of consumers if the business has actual knowledge that the consumer is less than 16 years of age, unless the consumer, in the case of consumers between 13 and 16 years of age, or the consumer's parent or guardian, in the case of consumers who are less than 13 years of age, has affirmatively authorized the sale of the consumer's personal information. A business that willfully disregards the consumer's age shall be deemed to have had actual knowledge of the consumer's age. This right may be referred to as the "right to opt in."

1798.125.

> (a) (1) A business shall not discriminate against a consumer because the consumer exercised any of the consumer's rights under this title, including, but not limited to, by:

> > (A) Denying goods or services to the consumer.

(B) Charging different prices or rates for goods or services, including through the use of discounts or other benefits or imposing penalties.

(C) Providing a different level or quality of goods or services to the consumer, if the consumer exercises the consumer's rights under this title.

(D) Suggesting that the consumer will receive a different price or rate for goods or services or a different level or quality of goods or services.

(2) Nothing in this subdivision prohibits a business from charging a consumer a different price or rate, or from providing a different level or quality of goods or services to the consumer, if that difference is reasonably related to the value provided to the consumer by the consumer's data.

(b) (1) A business may offer financial incentives, including payments to consumers as compensation, for the collection of personal information, the sale of personal information, or the deletion of personal information. A business may also offer a different price, rate, level, or quality of goods or services to the consumer if that price or difference is directly related to the value provided to the consumer by the consumer's data.

(2) A business that offers any financial incentives pursuant to subdivision (a), shall notify consumers of the financial incentives pursuant to Section 1798.135.

(3) A business may enter a consumer into a financial incentive program only if the consumer gives the business prior opt-in consent pursuant to Section 1798.135 which clearly describes the material terms of the financial incentive program, and which may be revoked by the consumer at any time.

(4) A business shall not use financial incentive practices that are unjust, unreasonable, coercive, or usurious in nature.

Section 1798.130.

(a) In order to comply with Sections 1798.100, 1798.105, 1798.110, 1798.115, and 1798.125, in a form that is reasonably accessible to consumers, a business shall:

(1) Make available to consumers two or more designated methods for submitting requests for information required to be disclosed pursuant to Sections 1798.110 and 1798.115, including, at a minimum, a toll-free telephone number, and if the business maintains an Internet Web site, a Web site address.

(2) Disclose and deliver the required information to a consumer free of charge within 45 days of receiving a verifiable request from the consumer. The business shall promptly take steps to determine whether the request is a verifiable request, but this shall not extend the business's duty to disclose and deliver the information within 45 days of receipt of the consumer's request. The time period to provide the required information may be extended once by an additional 45 days when reasonably necessary, provided the consumer is provided notice of the extension within the first 45-day period. The disclosure shall cover the 12-month period preceding the business's receipt of the verifiable request and shall be made in writing and delivered through the consumer's account with the business, if the consumer

maintains an account with the business, or by mail or electronically at the consumer's option if the consumer does not maintain an account with the business, in a readily useable format that allows the consumer to transmit this information from one entity to another entity without hindrance. The business shall not require the consumer to create an account with the business in order to make a verifiable request.

(3) For purposes of subdivision (b) of Section 1798.110:

> (A) To identify the consumer, associate the information provided by the consumer in the verifiable request to any personal information previously collected by the business about the consumer.

> (B) Identify by category or categories the personal information collected about the consumer in the preceding 12 months by reference to the enumerated category or categories in subdivision (c) that most closely describes the personal information collected.

(4) For purposes of subdivision (b) of Section 1798.115:

> (A) Identify the consumer and associate the information provided by the consumer in the verifiable request to any personal information previously collected by the business about the consumer.

> (B) Identify by category or categories the personal information of the consumer that the business sold in the preceding 12 months by reference to the enumerated category in subdivision (c) that most closely describes the personal information, and provide the categories of third parties to whom the consumer's personal information was sold in the preceding 12 months by reference to the enumerated category or categories in subdivision (c) that most closely describes the personal information sold. The business shall disclose the information in a list that is separate from a list generated for the purposes of subparagraph (C).

> (C) Identify by category or categories the personal information of the consumer that the business disclosed for a business purpose in the preceding 12 months by reference to the enumerated category or categories in subdivision (c) that most closely describes the personal information, and provide the categories of third parties to whom the consumer's personal information was disclosed for a business purpose in the preceding 12 months by reference to the enumerated category or categories in subdivision (c) that most closely describes the personal information disclosed. The business shall disclose the information in a list that is separate from a list generated for the purposes of subparagraph (B).

(5) Disclose the following information in its online privacy policy or policies if the business has an online privacy policy or policies and in any California-specific description of consumers' privacy rights, or if the business does not maintain those policies, on its Internet Web site, and update that information at least once every 12 months:

> (A) A description of a consumer's rights pursuant to Sections 1798.110, 1798.115, and 1798.125 and one or more designated methods for submitting requests.

(B) For purposes of subdivision (c) of Section 1798.110, a list of the categories of personal information it has collected about consumers in the preceding 12 months by reference to the enumerated category or categories in subdivision (c) that most closely describe the personal information collected.

(C) For purposes of paragraphs (1) and (2) of subdivision (c) of Section 1798.115, two separate lists:

(i) A list of the categories of personal information it has sold about consumers in the preceding 12 months by reference to the enumerated category or categories in subdivision (c) that most closely describe the personal information sold, or if the business has not sold consumers' personal information in the preceding 12 months, the business shall disclose that fact.

(ii) A list of the categories of personal information it has disclosed about consumers for a business purpose in the preceding 12 months by reference to the enumerated category in subdivision (c) that most closely describe the personal information disclosed, or if the business has not disclosed consumers' personal information for a business purpose in the preceding 12 months, the business shall disclose that fact.

(6) Ensure that all individuals responsible for handling consumer inquiries about the business's privacy practices or the business's compliance with this title are informed of all requirements in Sections 1798.110, 1798.115, 1798.125, and this section, and how to direct consumers to exercise their rights under those sections.

(7) Use any personal information collected from the consumer in connection with the business's verification of the consumer's request solely for the purposes of verification.

(b) A business is not obligated to provide the information required by Sections 1798.110 and 1798.115 to the same consumer more than twice in a 12-month period.

(c) The categories of personal information required to be disclosed pursuant to Sections 1798.110 and 1798.115 shall follow the definition of personal information in Section 1798.140.

Section 1798.135.

(a) A business that is required to comply with Section 1798.120 shall, in a form that is reasonably accessible to consumers:

(1) Provide a clear and conspicuous link on the business' Internet homepage, titled "Do Not Sell My Personal Information," to an Internet Web page that enables a consumer, or a person authorized by the consumer, to opt out of the sale of the consumer's personal information. A business shall not require a consumer to create an account in order to direct the business not to sell the consumer's personal information.

(2) Include a description of a consumer's rights pursuant to Section 1798.120, along with a separate link to the "Do Not Sell My Personal Information" Internet Web page in:

(A) Its online privacy policy or policies if the business has an online privacy policy or policies.

(B) Any California-specific description of consumers' privacy rights.

(3) Ensure that all individuals responsible for handling consumer inquiries about the business's privacy practices or the business's compliance with this title are informed of all requirements in Section 1798.120 and this section and how to direct consumers to exercise their rights under those sections.

(4) For consumers who exercise their right to opt out of the sale of their personal information, refrain from selling personal information collected by the business about the consumer.

(5) For a consumer who has opted out of the sale of the consumer's personal information, respect the consumer's decision to opt out for at least 12 months before requesting that the consumer authorize the sale of the consumer's personal information.

(6) Use any personal information collected from the consumer in connection with the submission of the consumer's opt-out request solely for the purposes of complying with the opt-out request.

(b) Nothing in this title shall be construed to require a business to comply with the title by including the required links and text on the homepage that the business makes available to the public generally, if the business maintains a separate and additional homepage that is dedicated to California consumers and that includes the required links and text, and the business takes reasonable steps to ensure that California consumers are directed to the homepage for California consumers and not the homepage made available to the public generally.

(c) A consumer may authorize another person solely to opt out of the sale of the consumer's personal information on the consumer's behalf, and a business shall comply with an opt out request received from a person authorized by the consumer to act on the consumer's behalf, pursuant to regulations adopted by the Attorney General.

Section 1798.140. For purposes of this title:

(a) "Aggregate consumer information" means information that relates to a group or category of consumers, from which individual consumer identities have been removed, that is not linked or reasonably linkable to any consumer or household, including via a device. "Aggregate consumer information" does not mean one or more individual consumer records that have been de-identified.

(b) "Biometric information" means an individual's physiological, biological or behavioral characteristics, including an individual's deoxyribonucleic acid (DNA), that can be used, singly or in combination with each other or with other identifying data, to establish individual identity. Biometric information includes, but is not limited to, imagery of the iris, retina, fingerprint, face, hand, palm, vein patterns, and voice recordings, from which an identifier template, such as a faceprint, a minutiae template, or a voiceprint, can be extracted, and keystroke patterns or rhythms, gait patterns or rhythms, and sleep, health, or exercise data that contain identifying information.

(c) "Business" means:

(1) A sole proprietorship, partnership, limited liability company, corporation, association, or other legal entity that is organized or operated for the profit or financial benefit of its shareholders or other owners, that collects consumers' personal information, or on the behalf of which such information is collected

and that alone, or jointly with others, determines the purposes and means of the processing of consumers' personal information, that does business in the State of California, and that satisfies one or more of the following thresholds:

(A) Has annual gross revenues in excess of twenty-five million dollars ($25,000,000), as adjusted pursuant to paragraph (5) of subdivision (a) of Section 1798.185.

(B) Alone or in combination, annually buys, receives for the business' commercial purposes, sells, or shares for commercial purposes, alone or in combination, the personal information of 50,000 or more consumers, households, or devices.

(C) Derives 50 percent or more of its annual revenues from selling consumers' personal information.

(2) Any entity that controls or is controlled by a business, as defined in paragraph (1), and that shares common branding with the business. "Control" or "controlled" means ownership of, or the power to vote, more than 50 percent of the outstanding shares of any class of voting security of a business; control in any manner over the election of a majority of the directors, or of individuals exercising similar functions; or the power to exercise a controlling influence over the management of a company. "Common branding" means a shared name, servicemark, or trademark.

(d) "Business purpose" means the use of personal information for the business' or a service provider's operational purposes, or other notified purposes, provided that the use of personal information shall be reasonably necessary and proportionate to achieve the operational purpose for which the personal information was collected or processed or for another operational purpose that is compatible with the context in which the personal information was collected. Business purposes are:

(1) Auditing related to a current interaction with the consumer and concurrent transactions, including, but not limited to, counting ad impressions to unique visitors, verifying positioning and quality of ad impressions, and auditing compliance with this specification and other standards.

(2) Detecting security incidents, protecting against malicious, deceptive, fraudulent, or illegal activity, and prosecuting those responsible for that activity.

(3) Debugging to identify and repair errors that impair existing intended functionality.

(4) Short-term, transient use, provided the personal information that is not disclosed to another third party and is not used to build a profile about a consumer or otherwise alter an individual consumer's experience outside the current interaction, including, but not limited to, the contextual customization of ads shown as part of the same interaction.

(5) Performing services on behalf of the business or service provider, including maintaining or servicing accounts, providing customer service, processing or fulfilling orders and transactions, verifying customer information, processing payments, providing financing, providing advertising or marketing services, providing analytic services, or providing similar services on behalf of the business or service provider.

(6) Undertaking internal research for technological development and demonstration.

(7) Undertaking activities to verify or maintain the quality or safety of a service or device that is owned, manufactured, manufactured for, or controlled by the business, and to improve, upgrade, or enhance the service or device that is owned, manufactured, manufactured for, or controlled by the business.

(e) "Collects," "collected," or "collection" means buying, renting, gathering, obtaining, receiving, or accessing any personal information pertaining to a consumer by any means. This includes receiving information from the consumer, either actively or passively, or by observing the consumer's behavior.

(f) "Commercial purposes" means to advance a person's commercial or economic interests, such as by inducing another person to buy, rent, lease, join, subscribe to, provide, or exchange products, goods, property, information, or services, or enabling or effecting, directly or indirectly, a commercial transaction. "Commercial purposes" do not include for the purpose of engaging in speech that state or federal courts have recognized as noncommercial speech, including political speech and journalism.

(g) "Consumer" means a natural person who is a California resident, as defined in Section 17014 of Title 18 of the California Code of Regulations, as that section read on September 1, 2017, however identified, including by any unique identifier.

(h) "Deidentified" means information that cannot reasonably identify, relate to, describe, be capable of being associated with, or be linked, directly or indirectly, to a particular consumer, provided that a business that uses deidentified information:

(1) Has implemented technical safeguards that prohibit reidentification of the consumer to whom the information may pertain.

(2) Has implemented business processes that specifically prohibit reidentification of the information.

(3) Has implemented business processes to prevent inadvertent release of deidentified information.

(4) Makes no attempt to reidentify the information.

(i) "Designated methods for submitting requests" means a mailing address, email address, Internet Web page, Internet Web portal, toll-free telephone number, or other applicable contact information, whereby consumers may submit a request or direction under this title, and any new, consumer-friendly means of contacting a business, as approved by the Attorney General pursuant to Section 1798.185.

(j) "Device" means any physical object that is capable of connecting to the Internet, directly or indirectly, or to another device.

(k) "Health insurance information" means a consumer's insurance policy number or subscriber identification number, any unique identifier used by a health insurer to identify the consumer, or any information in the consumer's application and claims history, including any appeals records, if the information is linked or reasonably linkable to a consumer or household, including via a device, by a business or service provider.

(l) "Homepage" means the introductory page of an Internet Web site and any Internet Web page where personal information is collected. In the case of an online service, such as a mobile application, homepage means the application's platform page or download page, a link within the application, such as from the application configuration, "About," "Information," or settings page, and any other location that allows consumers to review the notice required by subdivision (a) of Section 1798.145, including, but not limited to, before downloading the application.

(m) "Infer" or "inference" means the derivation of information, data, assumptions, or conclusions from facts, evidence, or another source of information or data.

(n) "Person" means an individual, proprietorship, firm, partnership, joint venture, syndicate, business trust, company, corporation, limited liability company, association, committee, and any other organization or group of persons acting in concert.

(o)     (1) "Personal information" means information that identifies, relates to, describes, is capable of being associated with, or could reasonably be linked, directly or indirectly, with a particular consumer or household. Personal information includes, but is not limited to, the following:

>     (A) Identifiers such as a real name, alias, postal address, unique personal identifier, online identifier Internet Protocol address, email address, account name, social security number, driver's license number, passport number, or other similar identifiers.

>     (B) Any categories of personal information described in subdivision (e) of Section 1798.80.

>     (C) Characteristics of protected classifications under California or federal law.

>     (D) Commercial information, including records of personal property, products or services purchased, obtained, or considered, or other purchasing or consuming histories or tendencies.

>     (E) Biometric information.

>     (F) Internet or other electronic network activity information, including, but not limited to, browsing history, search history, and information regarding a consumer's interaction with an Internet Web site, application, or advertisement.

>     (G) Geolocation data.

>     (H) Audio, electronic, visual, thermal, olfactory, or similar information.

>     (I) Professional or employment-related information.

>     (J) Education information, defined as information that is not publicly available personally identifiable information as defined in the Family Educational Rights and Privacy Act (20 U.S.C. section 1232g, 34 C.F.R. Part 99).

>     (K) Inferences drawn from any of the information identified in this subdivision to create a profile about a consumer reflecting the consumer's preferences, characteristics, psychological trends, preferences, predispositions, behavior, attitudes, intelligence, abilities, and aptitudes.

(2) "Personal information" does not include publicly available information. For these purposes, "publicly available" means information that is lawfully made available from federal, state, or local

government records, if any conditions associated with such information. "Publicly available" does not mean biometric information collected by a business about a consumer without the consumer's knowledge. Information is not "publicly available" if that data is used for a purpose that is not compatible with the purpose for which the data is maintained and made available in the government records or for which it is publicly maintained. "Publicly available" does not include consumer information that is deidentified or aggregate consumer information.

(p) "Probabilistic identifier" means the identification of a consumer or a device to a degree of certainty of more probable than not based on any categories of personal information included in, or similar to, the categories enumerated in the definition of personal information.

(q) "Processing" means any operation or set of operations that are performed on personal data or on sets of personal data, whether or not by automated means.

(r) "Pseudonymize" or "Pseudonymization" means the processing of personal information in a manner that renders the personal information no longer attributable to a specific consumer without the use of additional information, provided that the additional information is kept separately and is subject to technical and organizational measures to ensure that the personal information is not attributed to an identified or identifiable consumer.

(s) "Research" means scientific, systematic study and observation, including basic research or applied research that is in the public interest and that adheres to all other applicable ethics and privacy laws or studies conducted in the public interest in the area of public health. Research with personal information that may have been collected from a consumer in the course of the consumer's interactions with a business' service or device for other purposes shall be:

(1) Compatible with the business purpose for which the personal information was collected.

(2) Subsequently pseudonymized and deidentified, or deidentified and in the aggregate, such that the information cannot reasonably identify, relate to, describe, be capable of being associated with, or be linked, directly or indirectly, to a particular consumer.

(3) Made subject to technical safeguards that prohibit reidentification of the consumer to whom the information may pertain.

(4) Subject to business processes that specifically prohibit reidentification of the information.

(5) Made subject to business processes to prevent inadvertent release of deidentified information.

(6) Protected from any reidentification attempts.

(7) Used solely for research purposes that are compatible with the context in which the personal information was collected.

(8) Not be used for any commercial purpose.

(9) Subjected by the business conducting the research to additional security controls limit access to the research data to only those individuals in a business as are necessary to carry out the research purpose.

(t)        (1) "Sell," "selling," "sale," or "sold," means selling, renting, releasing, disclosing, disseminating, making available, transferring, or otherwise communicating orally, in writing, or by electronic or other means, a consumer's personal information by the business to another business or a third party for monetary or other valuable consideration.

(2) For purposes of this title, a business does not sell personal information when:

(A) A consumer uses or directs the business to intentionally disclose personal information or uses the business to intentionally interact with a third party, provided the third party does not also sell the personal information, unless that disclosure would be consistent with the provisions of this title. An intentional interaction occurs when the consumer intends to interact with the third party, via one or more deliberate interactions. Hovering over, muting, pausing, or closing a given piece of content does not constitute a consumer's intent to interact with a third party.

(B) The business uses or shares an identifier for a consumer who has opted out of the sale of the consumer's personal information for the purposes of alerting third parties that the consumer has opted out of the sale of the consumer's personal information.

(C) The business uses or shares with a service provider personal information of a consumer that is necessary to perform a business purposes if both of the following conditions are met: services that the service provider performs on the business' behalf, provided that the service provider also does not sell the personal information.

(i) The business has provided notice that information being used or shared in its terms and conditions consistent with Section 1798.135.

(ii) The service provider does not further collect, sell, or use the personal information of the consumer except as necessary to perform the business purpose.

(D) The business transfers to a third party the personal information of a consumer as an asset that is part of a merger, acquisition, bankruptcy, or other transaction in which the third party assumes control of all or part of the business provided that information is used or shared consistently with Sections 1798.110 and 1798.115. If a third party materially alters how it uses or shares the personal information of a consumer in a manner that is materially inconsistent with the promises made at the time of collection, it shall provide prior notice of the new or changed practice to the consumer. The notice shall be sufficiently prominent and robust to ensure that existing consumers can easily exercise their choices consistently with Section 1798.120. This subparagraph does not authorize a business to make material, retroactive privacy policy changes or make other changes in their privacy policy in a manner that would violate the Unfair and Deceptive Practices Act (Chapter 5 (commencing with Section 17200) of Part 2 of Division 7 of the Business and Professions Code).

(u) "Service" or "services" means work, labor, and services, including services furnished in connection with the sale or repair of goods.

(v) "Service provider" means a sole proprietorship, partnership, limited liability company, corporation, association, or other legal entity that is organized or operated for the profit or financial benefit of its shareholders or other owners, that processes information on behalf of a business and to which the business discloses a consumer's personal information for a business purpose pursuant to a written contract, provided that the contract prohibits the entity receiving the information from retaining, using, or disclosing the personal information for any purpose other than for the specific purpose of performing the services specified in the contract for the business, or as otherwise permitted by this title, including retaining, using, or disclosing the personal information for a commercial purpose other than providing the services specified in the contract with the business.

(w) "Third party" means a person who is not any of the following:

(1) The business that collects personal information from consumers under this title.

(2) A person to whom the business discloses a consumer's personal information for a business purpose pursuant to a written contract, provided that the contract:

(A) Prohibits the person receiving the personal information from:

(i) Selling the personal information.

(ii) Retaining, using, or disclosing the personal information for any purpose other than for the specific purpose of performing the services specified in the contract, including retaining, using, or disclosing the personal information for a commercial purpose other than providing the services specified in the contract.

(iii) Retaining, using, or disclosing the information outside of the direct business relationship between the person and the business.

(B) Includes a certification made by the person receiving the personal information that the person understands the restrictions in subparagraph (A) and will comply with them.

A person covered by paragraph (2) that violates any of the restrictions set forth in this title shall be liable for the violations. A business that discloses personal information to a person covered by paragraph (2) in compliance with paragraph (2) shall not be liable under this title if the person receiving the personal information uses it in violation of the restrictions set forth in this title, provided that, at the time of disclosing the personal information, the business does not have actual knowledge, or reason to believe, that the person intends to commit such a violation.

(x) "Unique identifier" or "Unique personal identifier" means a persistent identifier that can be used to recognize a consumer, a family, or a device that is linked to a consumer or family, over time and across different services, including, but not limited to, a device identifier; an Internet Protocol address; cookies, beacons, pixel tags, mobile ad identifiers, or similar technology; customer number, unique pseudonym, or user alias; telephone numbers, or other forms of persistent or probabilistic identifiers that can be used to identify a particular consumer or device. For purposes of this subdivision, "family" means a custodial parent or guardian and any minor children over which the parent or guardian has custody.

(y) "Verifiable consumer request" means a request that is made by a consumer, by a consumer on behalf of the consumer's minor child, or by a natural person or a person registered with the Secretary of State, authorized by the consumer to act on the consumer's behalf, and that the business can reasonably verify, pursuant to regulations adopted by the Attorney General pursuant to paragraph (7) of subdivision (a) of Section 1798.185 to be the consumer about whom the business has collected personal information. A business is not obligated to provide information to the consumer pursuant to Sections 1798.110 and 1798.115 if the business cannot verify, pursuant this subdivision and regulations adopted by the Attorney General pursuant to paragraph (7) of subdivision (a) of Section 1798.185, that the consumer making the request is the consumer about whom the business has collected information or is a person authorized by the consumer to act on such consumer's behalf.

Section 1798.145.

(a) The obligations imposed on businesses by this title shall not restrict a business's ability to:

(1) Comply with federal, state, or local laws.

(2) Comply with a civil, criminal, or regulatory inquiry, investigation, subpoena, or summons by federal, state, or local authorities.

(3) Cooperate with law enforcement agencies concerning conduct or activity that the business, service provider, or third party reasonably and in good faith believes may violate federal, state, or local law.

(4) Exercise or defend legal claims.

(5) Collect, use, retain, sell, or disclose consumer information that is deidentified or in the aggregate consumer information.

(6) Collect or sell a consumer's personal information if every aspect of that commercial conduct takes place wholly outside of California. For purposes of this title, commercial conduct takes place wholly outside of California if the business collected that information while the consumer was outside of California, no part of the sale of the consumer's personal information occurred in California, and no personal information collected while the consumer was in California is sold. This paragraph shall not permit a business from storing, including on a device, personal information about a consumer when the consumer is in California and then collecting that personal information when the consumer and stored personal information is outside of California.

(b) The obligations imposed on businesses by Sections 1798.110 to 1798.135, inclusive, shall not apply where compliance by the business with the title would violate an evidentiary privilege under California law and shall not prevent a business from providing the personal information of a consumer to a person covered by an evidentiary privilege under California law as part of a privileged communication.

(c) This act shall not apply to protected or health information that is collected by a covered entity governed by the Confidentiality of Medical Information Act (Part 2.6 (commencing with Section 56 of Division 1)) or governed by the privacy, security, and breach notification rules issued by the federal Department of Health and Human Services, Parts 160 and 164 of Title 45 of the Code of Federal Regulations, established pursuant to the Health Insurance Portability and Availability Act of 1996. For purposes of this subdivision, the definition of "medical information" in Section 56.05 shall apply and the definitions of "protected health information" and "covered entity" from the federal privacy rule shall apply.

(d) This title shall not apply to the sale of personal information to or from a consumer reporting agency if that information is to be reported in, or used to generate, a consumer report as defined by subdivision (d) of Section 1681a of Title 15 of the United States Code, and use of that information is limited by the federal Fair Credit Reporting Act (15 U.S.C. Sec. 1681 et seq.).

(e) This title shall not apply to personal information collected, processed, sold, or disclosed pursuant to the federal Gramm-Leach-Bliley Act (Public Law 106-102), and implementing regulations, if it is in conflict with that law.

(f) This title shall not apply to personal information collected, processed, sold, or disclosed pursuant to the Driver's Privacy Protection Act of 1994 (18 U.S.C. Sec. 2721 et seq.), if it is in conflict with that act.

(g) Notwithstanding a business' obligations to respond to and honor consumer rights requests pursuant to this title:

> (1) A time period for a business to respond to any verified consumer request may be extended by up to 90 additional days where necessary, taking into account the complexity and number of the requests. The business shall inform the consumer of any such extension within 45 days of receipt of the request, together with the reasons for the delay.

> (2) If the business does not take action on the request of the consumer, the business shall inform the consumer, without delay and at the latest within the time period permitted of response by this section, of the reasons for not taking action and any rights the consumer may have to appeal the decision to the business.

> (3) If requests from a consumer are manifestly unfounded or excessive, in particular because of their repetitive character, a business may either charge a reasonable fee, taking into account the administrative costs of providing the information or communication or taking the action requested, or refuse to act on the request and notify the consumer of the reason for refusing the request. The business shall bear the burden of demonstrating that any verified consumer request is manifestly unfounded or excessive.

(h) A business that discloses personal information to a service provider shall not be liable under this title if the service provider receiving the personal information uses it in violation of the restrictions set forth in the title, provided that, at the time of disclosing the personal information, the business does not have actual knowledge, or reason to believe, that the service provider intends to commit such a violation. A service provider shall likewise not be liable under this title for the obligations of a business for which it provides services as set forth in this title.

(i) This title shall not be construed to require a business to reidentify or otherwise link information that is not maintained in a manner that would be considered personal information.

(j) The rights afforded to consumers and the obligations imposed on the business in this title shall not adversely affect the rights and freedoms of other consumers.

Section 1798.150.

(a)　　(1) Any consumer whose nonencrypted or nonredacted personal information, as defined in subparagraph (A) of paragraph (1) of subdivision (d) of Section 1798.81.5, is subject to an unauthorized access and exfiltration, theft, or disclosure as a result of the business' violation of the duty to implement and maintain reasonable security procedures and practices appropriate to the nature of the information to protect the personal information may institute a civil action for any of the following:

> (A) To recover damages in an amount not less than one hundred dollars ($100) and not greater than seven hundred and fifty ($750) per consumer per incident or actual damages, whichever is greater.

> (B) Injunctive or declaratory relief.

> (C) Any other relief the court deems proper.

> (2) In assessing the amount of statutory damages, the court shall consider any one or more of the relevant circumstances presented by any of the parties to the case, including, but not limited to, the nature and seriousness of the misconduct, the number of violations, the persistence of the misconduct, the length of time over which the misconduct occurred, the willfulness of the defendant's misconduct, and the defendant's assets, liabilities, and net worth.

(b) Actions pursuant to this section may be brought by a consumer if all of the following requirements are met:

> (1) Prior to initiating any action against a business for statutory damages on an individual or class-wide basis, a consumer shall provide a business 30 days' written notice identifying the specific provisions of this title the consumer alleges have been or are being violated. In the event a cure is possible, if within the 30 days the business actually cures the noticed violation and provides the consumer an express written statement that the violations have been cured and that no further violations shall occur, no action for individual statutory damages or class-wide statutory damages may be initiated against the business. No notice shall be required prior to an individual consumer initiating an action solely for actual pecuniary damages suffered as a result of the alleged violations of this title. If a business continues to violate this title in breach of the express written statement provided to the consumer under this section, the consumer may initiate an action against the business to enforce the written statement and may pursue statutory damages for each breach of the express written statement, as well as any other violation of the title that postdates the written statement.

> (2) A consumer bringing an action as defined in paragraph (1) of subdivision (c) shall notify the Attorney General within 30 days that the action has been filed.

> (3) The Attorney General, upon receiving such notice shall, within 30 days, do one of the following:

> > (A) Notify the consumer bringing the action of the Attorney General's intent to prosecute an action against the violation. If the Attorney General does not prosecute within six months, the consumer may proceed with the action.

> > (B) Refrain from acting within the 30 days, allowing the consumer bringing the action to proceed.

(C) Notify the consumer bringing the action that the consumer shall not proceed with the action.

(c) Nothing in this act shall be interpreted to serve as the basis for a private right of action under any other law. This shall not be construed to relieve any party from any duties or obligations imposed under other law or the United States or California Constitution.

Section 1798.155. Any business or third party may seek the opinion of the Attorney General for guidance on how to comply with the provisions of this title.

(a) A business shall be in violation of this title if it fails to cure any alleged violation within 30 days after being notified of alleged noncompliance. Any business, service provider, or other person that violates this title shall be liable for a civil penalty as provided in Section 17206 of the Business and Professions Code in a civil action brought in the name of the people of the State of California by the Attorney General. The civil penalties provided for in this section shall be exclusively assessed and recovered in a civil action brought in the name of the people of the State of California by the Attorney General.

(b) Notwithstanding Section 17206 of the Business and Professions Code, any person, business, or service provider that intentionally violates this title may be liable for a civil penalty of up to seven thousand five hundred dollars ($7,500) for each violation.

(c) Notwithstanding Section 17206 of the Business and Professions Code, any civil penalty assessed pursuant to Section 17206 for a violation of this title, and the proceeds of any settlement of an action brought pursuant to subdivision (a), shall be allocated as follows:

(1) Twenty percent to the Consumer Privacy Fund, created within the General Fund pursuant to subdivision (a) of Section 1798.109, with the intent to fully offset any costs incurred by the state courts and the Attorney General in connection with this title.

(2) Eighty percent to the jurisdiction on whose behalf the action leading to the civil penalty was brought.

(d) It is the intent of the Legislature that the percentages specified in subdivision (c) be adjusted as necessary to ensure that any civil penalties assessed for a violation of this title fully offset any costs incurred by the state courts and the Attorney General in connection with this title, including a sufficient amount to cover any deficit from a prior fiscal year.

Section 1798.160.

(a) A special fund to be known as the "Consumer Privacy Fund" is hereby created within the General Fund in the State Treasury, and is available upon appropriation by the Legislature to offset any costs incurred by the state courts in connection with actions brought to enforce this title and any costs incurred by the Attorney General in carrying out the Attorney General's duties under this title.

(b) Funds transferred to the Consumer Privacy Fund shall be used exclusively to offset any costs incurred by the state courts and the Attorney General in connection with this title. These funds shall not be subject to appropriation or transfer by the Legislature for any other purpose, unless the Director of Finance determines that the funds are in excess of the funding needed to fully offset the costs incurred by the state courts and the Attorney General in connection with this title, in which case the Legislature may appropriate excess funds for other purposes.

Section 1798.175. This title is intended to further the constitutional right of privacy and to supplement existing laws relating to consumers' personal information, including, but not limited to, Chapter 22 (commencing with Section 22575) of Division 8 of the Business and Professions Code and Title 1.81 (commencing with Section 1798.80). The provisions of this title are not limited to information collected electronically or over the Internet, but apply to the collection and sale of all personal information collected by a business from consumers. Wherever possible, law relating to consumers' personal information should be construed to harmonize with the provisions of this title, but in the event of a conflict between other laws and the provisions of this title, the provisions of the law that afford the greatest protection for the right of privacy for consumers shall control.

Section 1798.180. This title is a matter of statewide concern and supersedes and preempts all rules, regulations, codes, ordinances, and other laws adopted by a city, county, city and county, municipality, or local agency regarding the collection and sale of consumers' personal information by a business.

Section 1798.185.

(a) On or before January 1, 2020, the Attorney General shall solicit broad public participation to adopt regulations to further the purposes of this title, including, but not limited to, the following areas:

> (1) Updating as needed additional categories of personal information to those enumerated in subdivision (c) of Section 1798.130 and subdivision (o) of Section 1798.140 in order to address changes in technology, data collection practices, obstacles to implementation, and privacy concerns.

> (2) Updating as needed the definition of unique identifiers to address changes in technology, data collection, obstacles to implementation, and privacy concerns, and additional categories to the definition of designated methods for submitting requests to facilitate a consumer's ability to obtain information from a business pursuant to Section 1798.130.

> (3) Establishing any exceptions necessary to comply with state or federal law, including, but not limited to, those relating to trade secrets and intellectual property rights, within one year of passage of this title and as needed thereafter.

> (4) Establishing rules and procedures for the following, within one year of passage of this title and as needed thereafter:

>> (A) To facilitate and govern the submission of a request by a consumer to opt out of the sale of personal information pursuant to paragraph (1) of subdivision (a) of Section 1798.145.

>> (B) To govern business compliance with a consumer's opt-out request.

>> (C) The development and use of a recognizable and uniform opt-out logo or button by all businesses to promote consumer awareness of the opportunity to opt out of the sale of personal information.

(5) Adjusting the monetary threshold in subparagraph (A) of paragraph (1) of subdivision (b) of Section 1798.106 in January of every odd-numbered year to reflect any increase in the Consumer Price Index.

(6) Establishing rules, procedures, and any exceptions necessary to ensure that the notices and information that businesses are required to provide pursuant to this title are provided in a manner that may be easily understood by the average consumer, are accessible to consumers with disabilities, and are available in the language primarily used to interact with the consumer, including establishing rules and guidelines regarding financial incentive offerings, within one year of passage of this title and as needed thereafter.

(7) Establishing rules and procedures to further the purposes of Sections 1798.110 and 1798.115 and to facilitate a consumer's or the consumer's authorized agent's ability to obtain information pursuant to Section 1798.130, with the goal of minimizing the administrative burden on consumers, taking into account available technology, security concerns, and the burden on the business, to govern a business' determination that a request for information received by a consumer is a verifiable request, including treating a request submitted through a password-protected account maintained by the consumer with the business while the consumer is logged into the account as a verifiable request and providing a mechanism for a consumer who does not maintain an account with the business to request information through the business' authentication of the consumer's identity, within one year of passage of this title and as needed thereafter.

(b) The Attorney General may adopt additional regulations as necessary to further the purposes of this title.

Section 1798.190. If a series of steps or transactions were component parts of a single transaction intended from the beginning to be taken with the intention of avoiding the reach of this title, including the disclosure of information by a business to a third party in order to avoid the definition of sell, a court shall disregard the intermediate steps or transactions for purposes of effectuating the purposes of this title.

Section 1798.192. Any provision of a contract or agreement of any kind that purports to waive or limit in any way a consumer's rights under this title, including, but not limited to, any right to a remedy or means of enforcement, shall be deemed contrary to public policy and shall be void and unenforceable. This section shall not prevent a consumer from declining to request information from a business, declining to opt out of a business' sale of the consumer's personal information, or authorizing a business to sell the consumer's personal information after previously opting out.

Section 1798.194. This title shall be liberally construed to effectuate its purposes.

Section 1798.196. This title is intended to supplement federal and state law, if permissible, but shall not apply if such application is preempted by, or in conflict with, federal law or the California Constitution.

Section 1798.198.

(a) Subject to limitation provided in subdivision (b), this title shall be operative January 1, 2020.

(b) This act shall become operative only if initiative measure No. 17-0039, The Consumer Right to Privacy Act of 2018, is withdrawn from the ballot pursuant to Section 9604 of the Elections Code.

SEC. 4. (a) The provisions of this bill are severable. If any provision of this bill or its application is held invalid, that invalidity shall not affect other provisions or applications that can be given effect without the invalid provision or application.

# CALIFORNIA SECURITY OF CONNECTED DEVICES LAW (2018)

1798.91.04.

(a) A manufacturer of a connected device shall equip the device with a reasonable security feature or features that are all of the following:

    (1) Appropriate to the nature and function of the device.

    (2) Appropriate to the information it may collect, contain, or transmit.

    (3) Designed to protect the device and any information contained therein from unauthorized access, destruction, use, modification, or disclosure.

(b) Subject to all of the requirements of subdivision (a), if a connected device is equipped with a means for authentication outside a local area network, it shall be deemed a reasonable security feature under subdivision (a) if either of the following requirements are met:

    (1) The preprogrammed password is unique to each device manufactured.

    (2) The device contains a security feature that requires a user to generate a new means of authentication before access is granted to the device for the first time.

1798.91.05.

For the purposes of this title, the following terms have the following meanings:

(a) "Authentication" means a method of verifying the authority of a user, process, or device to access resources in an information system.

(b) "Connected device" means any device, or other physical object that is capable of connecting to the Internet, directly or indirectly, and that is assigned an Internet Protocol address or Bluetooth address.

(c) "Manufacturer" means the person who manufactures, or contracts with another person to manufacture on the person's behalf, connected devices that are sold or offered for sale in California. For the purposes of this subdivision, a contract with another person to manufacture on the person's behalf does not include a contract only to purchase a connected device, or only to purchase and brand a connected device.

(d) "Security feature" means a feature of a device designed to provide security for that device.

(e) "Unauthorized access, destruction, use, modification, or disclosure" means access, destruction, use, modification, or disclosure that is not authorized by the consumer.

1798.91.06.

(a) This title shall not be construed to impose any duty upon the manufacturer of a connected device related to unaffiliated third-party software or applications that a user chooses to add to a connected device.

(b) This title shall not be construed to impose any duty upon a provider of an electronic store, gateway, marketplace, or other means of purchasing or downloading software or applications, to review or enforce compliance with this title.

(c) This title shall not be construed to impose any duty upon the manufacturer of a connected device to prevent a user from having full control over a connected device, including the ability to modify the software or firmware running on the device at the user's discretion.

(d) This title shall not apply to any connected device the functionality of which is subject to security requirements under federal law, regulations, or guidance promulgated by a federal agency pursuant to its regulatory enforcement authority.

(e) This title shall not be construed to provide a basis for a private right of action. The Attorney General, a city attorney, a county counsel, or a district attorney shall have the exclusive authority to enforce this title.

(f) The duties and obligations imposed by this title are cumulative with any other duties or obligations imposed under other law, and shall not be construed to relieve any party from any duties or obligations imposed under other law.

(g) This title shall not be construed to limit the authority of a law enforcement agency to obtain connected device information from a manufacturer as authorized by law or pursuant to an order of a court of competent jurisdiction.

(h) A covered entity, provider of health care, business associate, health care service plan, contractor, employer, or any other person subject to the federal Health Insurance Portability and Accountability Act of 1996 (HIPAA) (Public Law 104-191) or the Confidentiality of Medical Information Act (Part 2.6 (commencing with Section 56) of Division 1) shall not be subject to this title with respect to any activity regulated by those acts.

# Illinois Biometric Information Privacy Act (2008)

## 740 ILCS 14/1

§ 5. **Legislative findings**; intent. The General Assembly finds all of the following:

(a) The use of biometrics is growing in the business and security screening sectors and appears to promise streamlined financial transactions and security screenings.

(b) Major national corporations have selected the City of Chicago and other locations in this State as pilot testing sites for new applications of biometric-facilitated financial transactions, including finger-scan technologies at grocery stores, gas stations, and school cafeterias.

(c) Biometrics are unlike other unique identifiers that are used to access finances or other sensitive information. For example, social security numbers, when compromised, can be changed. Biometrics, however, are biologically unique to the individual; therefore, once compromised, the individual has no recourse, is at heightened risk for identity theft, and is likely to withdraw from biometric-facilitated transactions.

(d) An overwhelming majority of members of the public are weary of the use of biometrics when such information is tied to finances and other personal information.

(e) Despite limited State law regulating the collection, use, safeguarding, and storage of biometrics, many members of the public are deterred from partaking in biometric identifier-facilitated transactions.

(f) The full ramifications of biometric technology are not fully known.

(g) The public welfare, security, and safety will be served by regulating the collection, use, safeguarding, handling, storage, retention, and destruction of biometric identifiers and information.

§ 10. **Definitions**. In this Act:

"Biometric identifier" means a retina or iris scan, fingerprint, voiceprint, or scan of hand or face geometry. Biometric identifiers do not include writing samples, written signatures, photographs, human biological samples used for valid scientific testing or screening, demographic data, tattoo descriptions, or physical descriptions such as height, weight, hair color, or eye color. Biometric identifiers do not include donated organs, tissues, or parts as defined in the Illinois Anatomical Gift Act or blood or serum stored on behalf of recipients or potential recipients of living or cadaveric transplants and obtained or stored by a federally designated organ procurement agency. Biometric identifiers do not include biological materials regulated under the Genetic Information Privacy Act. Biometric identifiers do not include information captured from a patient in a health care setting or information collected, used, or stored for health care treatment, payment, or operations under the federal Health Insurance Portability and Accountability Act of 1996. Biometric identifiers do not include an X-ray, roentgen process, computed tomography, MRI, PET scan, mammography, or other image or film of the human anatomy used to diagnose, prognose, or treat an illness or other medical condition or to further validate scientific testing or screening.

"Biometric information" means any information, regardless of how it is captured, converted, stored, or shared, based on an individual's biometric identifier used to identify an individual. Biometric information does not include information derived from items or procedures excluded under the definition of biometric identifiers.

"Confidential and sensitive information" means personal information that can be used to uniquely identify an individual or an individual's account or property. Examples of confidential and sensitive information include, but are not limited to, a genetic marker, genetic testing information, a unique identifier number to locate an account or property, an account number, a PIN number, a pass code, a driver's license number, or a social security number.

"Private entity" means any individual, partnership, corporation, limited liability company, association, or other group, however organized. A private entity does not include a State or local government agency. A private entity does not include any court of Illinois, a clerk of the court, or a judge or justice thereof.

"Written release" means informed written consent or, in the context of employment, a release executed by an employee as a condition of employment.

## § 15. Retention; collection; disclosure; destruction.

(a) A private entity in possession of biometric identifiers or biometric information must develop a written policy, made available to the public, establishing a retention schedule and guidelines for permanently destroying biometric identifiers and biometric information when the initial purpose for collecting or obtaining such identifiers or information has been satisfied or within 3 years of the individual's last interaction with the private entity, whichever occurs first. Absent a valid warrant or subpoena issued by a court of competent jurisdiction, a private entity in possession of biometric identifiers or biometric information must comply with its established retention schedule and destruction guidelines.

(b) No private entity may collect, capture, purchase, receive through trade, or otherwise obtain a person's or a customer's biometric identifier or biometric information, unless it first:

(1) informs the subject or the subject's legally authorized representative in writing that a biometric identifier or biometric information is being collected or stored;

(2) informs the subject or the subject's legally authorized representative in writing of the specific purpose and length of term for which a biometric identifier or biometric information is being collected, stored, and used; and

(3) receives a written release executed by the subject of the biometric identifier or biometric information or the subject's legally authorized representative.

(c) No private entity in possession of a biometric identifier or biometric information may sell, lease, trade, or otherwise profit from a person's or a customer's biometric identifier or biometric information.

(d) No private entity in possession of a biometric identifier or biometric information may disclose, redisclose, or otherwise disseminate a person's or a customer's biometric identifier or biometric information unless:

(1) the subject of the biometric identifier or biometric information or the subject's legally authorized representative consents to the disclosure or redisclosure;

(2) the disclosure or redisclosure completes a financial transaction requested or authorized by the subject of the biometric identifier or the biometric information or the subject's legally authorized representative;

(3) the disclosure or redisclosure is required by State or federal law or municipal ordinance; or

(4) the disclosure is required pursuant to a valid warrant or subpoena issued by a court of competent jurisdiction.

(e) A private entity in possession of a biometric identifier or biometric information shall:

(1) store, transmit, and protect from disclosure all biometric identifiers and biometric information using the reasonable standard of care within the private entity's industry; and

(2) store, transmit, and protect from disclosure all biometric identifiers and biometric information in a manner that is the same as or more protective than the manner in which the private entity stores, transmits, and protects other confidential and sensitive information.

§ 20. **Right of action**. Any person aggrieved by a violation of this Act shall have a right of action in a State circuit court or as a supplemental claim in federal district court against an offending party. A prevailing party may recover for each violation:

(1) against a private entity that negligently violates a provision of this Act, liquidated damages of $1,000 or actual damages, whichever is greater;

(2) against a private entity that intentionally or recklessly violates a provision of this Act, liquidated damages of $5,000 or actual damages, whichever is greater;

(3) reasonable attorneys' fees and costs, including expert witness fees and other litigation expenses; and

(4) other relief, including an injunction, as the State or federal court may deem appropriate.

***

# Artificial Intelligence

# California Deepfake Law (2019)
California Civil Code §1708.86.

(a) For purposes of this section:

    (1) "Altered depiction" means a performance that was actually performed by the depicted individual but was subsequently altered to be in violation of this section.

    (2) "Authorized Representative" means an attorney, talent agent, or personal manager authorized to represent a depicted individual if the depicted individual is represented.

    (3) (A) "Consent" means an agreement written in plain language signed knowingly and voluntarily by the depicted individual that includes a general description of the sexually explicit material and the audiovisual work in which it will be incorporated.

        (B) A depicted individual may rescind consent by delivering written notice within three business days from the date consent was given to the person in whose favor consent was made, unless one of the following requirements is satisfied:

            (i) The depicted individual is given at least 72 hours to review the terms of the agreement before signing it.

            (ii) The depicted individual's authorized representative provides written approval of the signed agreement.

    (4) "Depicted individual" means an individual who appears, as a result of digitization, to be giving a performance they did not actually perform or to be performing in an altered depiction.

    (5) "Despicable conduct" means conduct that is so vile, base, or contemptible that it would be looked down on and despised by a reasonable person.

    (6) "Digitization" means to realistically depict any of the following:

        (A) The nude body parts of another human being as the nude body parts of the depicted individual.

        (B) Computer-generated nude body parts as the nude body parts of the depicted individual.

        (C) The depicted individual engaging in sexual conduct in which the depicted individual did not engage.

    (7) "Disclose" means to publish, make available, or distribute to the public.

    (8) "Individual" means a natural person.

    (9) "Malice" means that the defendant acted with intent to cause harm to the plaintiff or despicable conduct that was done with a willful and knowing disregard of the rights of the plaintiff. A person acts with knowing disregard within the meaning of this paragraph when they are aware of the probable harmful consequences of their conduct and deliberately fail to avoid those consequences.

    (10) "Nude" means visible genitals, pubic area, anus, or a female's postpubescent nipple or areola.

    (11) "Person" means a human being or legal entity.

    (12) "Plaintiff" includes cross-plaintiff.

    (13) "Sexual conduct" means any of the following:

        (A) Masturbation.

        (B) Sexual intercourse, including genital, oral, or anal, whether between persons regardless of sex or gender or between humans and animals.

        (C) Sexual penetration of the vagina or rectum by, or with, an object.

        (D) The transfer of semen by means of sexual conduct from the penis directly onto the depicted individual as a result of ejaculation.

(E) Sadomasochistic abuse involving the depicted individual.

(14) "Sexually explicit material" means any portion of an audiovisual work that shows the depicted individual performing in the nude or appearing to engage in, or being subjected to, sexual conduct.

(b) A depicted individual has a cause of action against a person who does either of the following:

(1) Creates and intentionally discloses sexually explicit material and the person knows or reasonably should have known the depicted individual in that material did not consent to its creation or disclosure.

(2) Intentionally discloses sexually explicit material that the person did not create and the person knows the depicted individual in that material did not consent to the creation of the sexually explicit material.

(c) (1) A person is not liable under this section in either of the following circumstances:

(A) The person discloses the sexually explicit material in the course of any of the following:

(i) Reporting unlawful activity.

(ii) Exercising the person's law enforcement duties.

(iii) Hearings, trials, or other legal proceedings.

(B) The material is any of the following:

(i) A matter of legitimate public concern.

(ii) A work of political or newsworthy value or similar work.

(iii) Commentary, criticism, or disclosure that is otherwise protected by the California Constitution or the United States Constitution.

(2) For purposes of this subdivision, sexually explicit material is not of newsworthy value solely because the depicted individual is a public figure.

(d) It shall not be a defense to an action under this section that there is a disclaimer included in the sexually explicit material that communicates that the inclusion of the depicted individual in the sexually explicit material was unauthorized or that the depicted individual did not participate in the creation or development of the material.

(e) (1) A prevailing plaintiff who suffers harm as a result of the violation of subdivision (b) may recover any of the following:

(A) An amount equal to the monetary gain made by the defendant from the creation, development, or disclosure of the sexually explicit material.

(B) One of the following:

(i) Economic and noneconomic damages proximately caused by the disclosure of the sexually explicit material, including damages for emotional distress.

(ii) Upon request of the plaintiff at any time before the final judgment is rendered, the plaintiff may instead recover an award of statutory damages for all unauthorized acts involved in the action, with respect to any one work, as follows:

(I) A sum of not less than one thousand five hundred dollars ($1,500) but not more than thirty thousand dollars ($30,000).

(II) If the unlawful act was committed with malice, the award of statutory damages may be increased to a maximum of one hundred fifty thousand dollars ($150,000).

(C) Punitive damages.

(D) Reasonable attorney's fees and costs.

(E) Any other available relief, including injunctive relief.

(2) The remedies provided by this section are cumulative and shall not be construed as restricting a remedy that is available under any other law.

(f) An action under this section shall be commenced no later than three years from the date the unauthorized creation, development, or disclosure was discovered or should have been discovered with the exercise of reasonable diligence.

(g) The provisions of this section are severable. If any provision of this section or its application is held invalid, that invalidity shall not affect other provisions.

# California Bot Disclosure Law (2018)

Chapter 6. Bots

17940. For purposes of this chapter:

(a) "Bot" means an automated online account where all or substantially all of the actions or posts of that account are not the result of a person.

(b) "Online" means appearing on any public-facing Internet Web site, Web application, or digital application, including a social network or publication.

(c) "Online platform" means any public-facing Internet Web site, Web application, or digital application, including a social network or publication, that has 10,000,000 or more unique monthly United States visitors or users for a majority of months during the preceding 12 months.

(d) "Person" means a natural person, corporation, limited liability company, partnership, joint venture, association, estate, trust, government, governmental subdivision or agency, or other legal entity or any combination thereof.

17941.    (a) It shall be unlawful for any person to use a bot to communicate or interact with another person in California online, with the intent to mislead the other person about its artificial identity for the purpose of knowingly deceiving the person about the content of the communication in order to incentivize a purchase or sale of goods or services in a commercial transaction or to influence a vote in an election. A person using a bot shall not be liable under this section if the person discloses that it is a bot.

(b) The disclosure required by this section shall be clear, conspicuous, and reasonably designed to inform persons with whom the bot communicates or interacts that it is a bot.

17942. (a) The duties and obligations imposed by this chapter are cumulative with any other duties or obligation imposed by any other law.

(b) The provisions of this chapter are severable. If any provision of this chapter or its application is held invalid, that invalidity shall not affect other provisions or applications that can be given effect without the invalid provision or application.

(c) This chapter does not impose a duty on service providers of online platforms, including, but not limited to, Web hosting and Internet service providers.

# Colorado Statute on Insurers' Use of External Consumer Data and Information Sources, Algorithms, and Predictive Models (2021)
### Colorado Revised Statutes § 10-3-1104.9

(1) In addition to the methods and practices prohibited pursuant to section 10-3-1104 (1)(f), an insurer shall not, with regard to any insurance practice:

(a) Unfairly discriminate based on race, color, national or ethnic origin, religion, sex, sexual orientation, disability, gender identity, or gender expression; or

(b) Pursuant to rules adopted by the commissioner, use any external consumer data and information sources, as well as any algorithms or predictive models that use external consumer data and information sources, in a way that unfairly discriminates based on race, color, national or ethnic origin, religion, sex, sexual orientation, disability, gender identity, or gender expression.

(2)     (a) The commissioner shall adopt rules for the implementation of this section.

(b) The commissioner shall engage in a stakeholder process prior to the adoption of rules for any type of insurance that includes carriers, producers, consumer representatives, and other interested parties. The commissioner shall hold stakeholder meetings for stakeholders of different types of insurance to ensure sufficient opportunity to consider factors and processes relevant to each type of insurance. The commissioner shall provide notice of stakeholder meetings on the division website, and stakeholder meetings shall be open to the public.

(3)     (a) After the stakeholder process described in subsection (2) of this section, the commissioner shall adopt rules for specific types of insurance, by insurance practice, which rules establish means by which an insurer may demonstrate, to the extent practicable, that it has tested whether its use of external consumer data and information sources, as well as algorithms or predictive models using external consumer data and information sources, unfairly discriminates based on race, color, national or ethnic origin, religion, sex, sexual orientation, disability, gender identity, or gender expression. The rules shall not become effective until January 1, 2023, at the earliest, for any type of insurance, and the commissioner shall consider solvency impacts, if any, to insurers in adopting the rules.

(b) Rules adopted pursuant to this section must require each insurer to:

(I) Provide information to the commissioner concerning the external consumer data and information sources used by the insurer in the development and implementation of algorithms and predictive models for a particular type of insurance and insurance practice;

(II) Provide an explanation of the manner in which the insurer uses external consumer data and information sources, as well as algorithms and predictive models using external consumer data and information sources, for the particular type of insurance and insurance practice;

(III) Establish and maintain a risk management framework or similar processes or procedures that are reasonably designed to determine, to the extent practicable, whether the insurer's use of external consumer data and information sources, as well as algorithms and predictive models using external consumer data and information sources, unfairly discriminates based on race, color, national or ethnic origin, religion, sex, sexual orientation, disability, gender identity, or gender expression;

(IV) Provide an assessment of the results of the risk management framework or similar processes or procedures and actions taken to minimize the risk of unfair discrimination, including ongoing monitoring; and

(V) Provide an attestation by one or more officers that the insurer has implemented the risk management framework or similar processes or procedures appropriately on a continuous basis.

(c) The rules adopted by the commissioner pursuant to this section must include provisions establishing:

(I) A reasonable period of time for insurers to remedy any unfairly discriminatory impact in an algorithm or predictive model; and

(II) The ability of insurers to use external consumer data and information sources, as well as algorithms or predictive models using external consumer data and information sources, that have been previously assessed by the division and found not to be unfairly discriminatory.

(d) Documents, materials, and other information in the possession or control of the division that are obtained by, created by, or disclosed to the commissioner or any other person pursuant to this section or any rules adopted pursuant to this section are recognized as proprietary and containing trade secrets. All such documents, materials, and other information are confidential and privileged; are not subject to disclosure under the "Colorado Open Records Act", part 2 of article 72 of title 24[1], or other open records, freedom of information, sunshine, or similar law of this state; are not subject to subpoena; and are not subject to discovery or admissible in evidence in any private civil action. However, the commissioner may use the documents, materials, or other information in the furtherance of any regulatory or legal action brought as part of the commissioner's official duties. The commissioner shall not otherwise make the documents, materials, or other information public without the prior written consent of the insurer from which the documents, materials, or other information was obtained. The commissioner may make data publicly available in an aggregated or de-identified format in a manner deemed appropriate by the commissioner.

(4) Pursuant to section 10-3-1106, the commissioner may examine and investigate an insurer's use of an external consumer data and information source, algorithm, or predictive model in any insurance practice. Insurers shall cooperate with the commissioner and the division in any examination or investigation under this section.

(5)      (a) In the report submitted by the department of regulatory agencies to the legislative committees of reference during the first two weeks of each regular legislative session, pursuant to part 2 of article 7 of title 2, the division shall include:

(I) Information concerning any rules adopted pursuant to this section;

(II) Information concerning any changes in insurance rates that have resulted from the prohibitions described in subsection (1) of this section;

(III) A summary of the stakeholder engagement process described in subsection (2)(b) of this section; and

(IV) A description of data sources, if any, discussed during the stakeholder engagement process, which data sources insurers may use to comply with this section. ***

(7) Nothing in this section:

(a) Requires an insurer to collect from an applicant or policyholder the race, color, national or ethnic origin, religion, sex, sexual orientation, disability, gender identity, or gender expression of an individual; or

(b) May be construed to:

I) Prohibit the use of, or require life, annuity, long-term care, or disability insurers to test, medical, family history, occupational, disability, or behavioral information related to a specific individual, which information, based on actuarially sound principles, has a direct relationship to mortality, morbidity, or longevity risk unless such information is otherwise included in the testing of an algorithm or predictive model that also uses external consumer data and information sources;

(II) Prohibit the use of, or require life, annuity, long-term care, or disability insurers to test, traditional underwriting factors being used for the exclusive purpose of determining insurable interest or eligibility for coverage unless such factors are otherwise included in the testing of an algorithm or predictive model that also uses external consumer data and information sources;

(III) Amend, modify, or supersede section 10-3-1104 (1)(f)(III) or (1)(f)(IV); or

(IV) Prohibit the use of or require the testing of longstanding and well-established common industry practices in settling claims or traditional underwriting practices unless such practices or factors are otherwise included in the testing of an algorithm or predictive model that also uses external consumer data and information sources.

(8) As used in this section, unless the context otherwise requires:

(a) "Algorithm" means a computational or machine learning process that informs human decision making in insurance practices.

(b)(I) "External consumer data and information source" means a data or an information source that is used by an insurer to supplement traditional underwriting or other insurance practices or to establish lifestyle indicators that are used in insurance practices. "External consumer data and information source" includes credit scores, social media habits, locations, purchasing habits, home ownership, educational attainment, occupation, licensures, civil judgments, and court records.

(II) The commissioner may promulgate rules to further define "external consumer data and information source" for particular lines of insurance and insurance practices.

(c) "Insurance practice" means marketing, underwriting, pricing, utilization management, reimbursement methodologies, and claims management in the transaction of insurance.

(d) "Predictive model" means a process of using mathematical and computational methods that examine current and historical data sets for underlying patterns and calculate the probability of an outcome.

(e) "Unfairly discriminate" and "unfair discrimination" include the use of one or more external consumer data and information sources, as well as algorithms or predictive models using external consumer data and information sources, that have a correlation to race, color, national or ethnic origin, religion, sex, sexual orientation, disability, gender identity, or gender expression, and that use results in a disproportionately negative outcome for such classification or classifications, which negative outcome exceeds the reasonable correlation to the underlying insurance practice, including losses and costs for underwriting.

# Illinois Artificial Intelligence Video Interview Act (2019)
## Public Act 101–260, H.B. 2557

§ 1. Short title. This Act may be cited as the Artificial Intelligence Video Interview Act.

§ 5. Disclosure of the use of artificial intelligence analysis. An employer that asks applicants to record video interviews and uses an artificial intelligence analysis of the applicant-submitted videos shall do all of the following when considering applicants for positions based in Illinois before asking applicants to submit video interviews:

(1) Notify each applicant before the interview that artificial intelligence may be used to analyze the applicant's video interview and consider the applicant's fitness for the position.

(2) Provide each applicant with information before the interview explaining how the artificial intelligence works and what general types of characteristics it uses to evaluate applicants.

(3) Obtain, before the interview, consent from the applicant to be evaluated by the artificial intelligence program as described in the information provided.

An employer may not use artificial intelligence to evaluate applicants who have not consented to the use of artificial intelligence analysis.

§ 10. Sharing videos limited. An employer may not share applicant videos, except with persons whose expertise or technology is necessary in order to evaluate an applicant's fitness for a position.

§ 15. Destruction of videos. Upon request from the applicant, employers, within 30 days after receipt of the request, must delete an applicant's interviews and instruct any other persons who received copies of the applicant video interviews to also delete the videos, including all electronically generated backup copies. Any other such person shall comply with the employer's instructions.

# Contracting in Cyberspace

# ELECTRONIC SIGNATURES IN GLOBAL & NATIONAL COMMERCE ACT (E-SIGN) (2000)

SEC. 101. GENERAL RULE OF VALIDITY.

(a) IN GENERAL- Notwithstanding any statute, regulation, or other rule of law (other than this title and title II), with respect to any transaction in or affecting interstate or foreign commerce—

> (1) a signature, contract, or other record relating to such transaction may not be denied legal effect, validity, or enforceability solely because it is in electronic form; and

> (2) a contract relating to such transaction may not be denied legal effect, validity, or enforceability solely because an electronic signature or electronic record was used in its formation.

(b) PRESERVATION OF RIGHTS AND OBLIGATIONS- This title does not—

* * *

> (2) require any person to agree to use or accept electronic records or electronic signatures, other than a governmental agency with respect to a record other than a contract to which it is a party.

(c) CONSUMER DISCLOSURES—

> (1) CONSENT TO ELECTRONIC RECORDS- Notwithstanding subsection (a), if a statute, regulation, or other rule of law requires that information relating to a transaction or transactions in or affecting interstate or foreign commerce be provided or made available to a consumer in writing, the use of an electronic record to provide or make available (whichever is required) such information satisfies the requirement that such information be in writing if—

> > (A) the consumer has affirmatively consented to such use and has not withdrawn such consent;

> > (B) the consumer, prior to consenting, is provided with a clear and conspicuous statement—

* * * informing the consumer of [right to withdraw consent, how to obtain a paper copy of the electronic record, etc.] * * * [and]

> > (C) the consumer—

> > > (i) prior to consenting, is provided with a statement of the hardware and software requirements for access to and retention of the electronic records; and

> > > (ii) consents electronically, or confirms his or her consent electronically, in a manner that reasonably demonstrates that the consumer can access information in the electronic form that will be used to provide the information that is the subject of the consent; and

* * *

(d) RETENTION OF CONTRACTS AND RECORDS-

(1) ACCURACY AND ACCESSIBILITY- If a statute, regulation, or other rule of law requires that a contract or other record relating to a transaction in or affecting interstate or foreign commerce be retained, that requirement is met by retaining an electronic record of the information in the contract or other record that—

(A) accurately reflects the information set forth in the contract or other record; and

(B) remains accessible to all persons who are entitled to access by statute, regulation, or rule of law, for the period required by such statute, regulation, or rule of law, in a form that is capable of being accurately reproduced for later reference, whether by transmission, printing, or otherwise.

\* \* \*

(e) ACCURACY AND ABILITY TO RETAIN CONTRACTS AND OTHER RECORDS- Notwithstanding subsection (a), if a statute, regulation, or other rule of law requires that a contract or other record relating to a transaction in or affecting interstate or foreign commerce be in writing, the legal effect, validity, or enforceability of an electronic record of such contract or other record may be denied if such electronic record is not in a form that is capable of being retained and accurately reproduced for later reference by all parties or persons who are entitled to retain the contract or other record.

\* \* \*

(h) ELECTRONIC AGENTS- A contract or other record relating to a transaction in or affecting interstate or foreign commerce may not be denied legal effect, validity, or enforceability solely because its formation, creation, or delivery involved the action of one or more electronic agents so long as the action of any such electronic agent is legally attributable to the person to be bound. \* \* \*

SEC. 103. SPECIFIC EXCEPTIONS.

(a) EXCEPTED REQUIREMENTS- The provisions of section 101 shall not apply to a contract or other record to the extent it is governed by—

(1) a statute, regulation, or other rule of law governing the creation and execution of wills, codicils, or testamentary trusts;

(2) a State statute, regulation, or other rule of law governing adoption, divorce, or other matters of family law; or

(3) the Uniform Commercial Code, as in effect in any State, other than sections 1-107 and 1-206 and Articles 2 and 2A.

SEC. 106. DEFINITIONS.

For purposes of this title:

\* \* \*

(4) ELECTRONIC RECORD. The term "electronic record" means a contract or other record created, generated, sent, communicated, received, or stored by electronic means.

(5) ELECTRONIC SIGNATURE. The term "electronic signature" means an electronic sound, symbol, or process, attached to or logically associated with a contract or other record and executed or adopted by a person with the intent to sign the record.

# UNIFORM ELECTRONIC TRANSACTIONS ACT (1999)
## *National Conference of Commissioners on Uniform State Laws*

### SECTION 2. DEFINITIONS. In this [Act]:

(1) "Agreement" means the bargain of the parties in fact, as found in their language or inferred from other circumstances and from rules, regulations, and procedures given the effect of agreements under laws otherwise applicable to a particular transaction.

(2) "Automated transaction" means a transaction conducted or performed, in whole or in part, by electronic means or electronic records, in which the acts or records of one or both parties are not reviewed by an individual in the ordinary course in forming a contract, performing under an existing contract, or fulfilling an obligation required by the transaction.

(3) "Computer program" means a set of statements or instructions to be used directly or indirectly in an information processing system in order to bring about a certain result.

(4) "Contract" means the total legal obligation resulting from the parties' agreement as affected by this [Act] and other applicable law.

(5) "Electronic" means relating to technology having electrical, digital, magnetic, wireless, optical, electromagnetic, or similar capabilities.

(6) "Electronic agent" means a computer program or an electronic or other automated means used independently to initiate an action or respond to electronic records or performances in whole or in part, without review or action by an individual.

(7) "Electronic record" means a record created, generated, sent, communicated, received, or stored by electronic means.

(8) "Electronic signature" means an electronic sound, symbol, or process attached to or logically associated with a record and executed or adopted by a person with the intent to sign the record.

(9) " Governmental agency" means an executive, legislative, or judicial agency, department, board, commission, authority, institution, or instrumentality of the federal government or of a State or of a county, municipality, or other political subdivision of a State.

(10) "Information" means data, text, images, sounds, codes, computer programs, software, databases, or the like.

(11) "Information processing system" means an electronic system for creating, generating, sending, receiving, storing, displaying, or processing information.

(12) "Person" means an individual, corporation, business trust, estate, trust, partnership, limited liability company, association, joint venture, governmental agency, public corporation, or any other legal or commercial entity.

(13) "Record" means information that is inscribed on a tangible medium or that is stored in an electronic or other medium and is retrievable in perceivable form.

(14) "Security procedure" means a procedure employed for the purpose of verifying that an electronic signature, record, or performance is that of a specific person or for detecting changes or errors in the information in an electronic record. The term includes a procedure that requires the use of algorithms or other codes, identifying words or numbers, encryption, or callback or other acknowledgment procedures.

(15) "State" means a State of the United States, the District of Columbia, Puerto Rico, the United States Virgin Islands, or any territory or insular possession subject to the jurisdiction of the United States. The term includes an Indian tribe or band, or Alaskan native village, which is recognized by federal law or formally acknowledged by a State.

(16) "Transaction" means an action or set of actions occurring between two or more persons relating to the conduct of business, commercial, or governmental affairs.

SECTION 3. SCOPE.

(a) Except as otherwise provided in subsection (b), this [Act] applies to electronic records and electronic signatures relating to a transaction.

(b) This [Act] does not apply to a transaction to the extent it is governed by:

> (1) a law governing the creation and execution of wills, codicils, or testamentary trusts;

> (2) [The Uniform Commercial Code other than Sections 1 107 and 1 206, Article 2, and Article 2A];

> (3) [the Uniform Computer Information Transactions Act]; and

> (4) [other laws, if any, identified by State].

SECTION 5. USE OF ELECTRONIC RECORDS AND ELECTRONIC SIGNATURES; VARIATION BY AGREEMENT.

(a) This [Act] does not require a record or signature to be created, generated, sent, communicated, received, stored, or otherwise processed or used by electronic means or in electronic form.

(b) This [Act] applies only to transactions between parties each of which has agreed to conduct transactions by electronic means. Whether the parties agree to conduct a transaction by electronic means is determined from the context and surrounding circumstances, including the parties' conduct.

Comments

Examples of circumstances from which it may be found that parties have reached an agreement to conduct transactions electronically include the following:

A. Automaker and supplier enter into a Trading Partner Agreement setting forth the terms, conditions and methods for the conduct of business between them electronically.

B. Joe gives out his business card with his business e mail address. It may be reasonable, under the circumstances, for a recipient of the card to infer that Joe has agreed to communicate electronically for business purposes. However, in the absence of additional facts, it would not necessarily be reasonable to infer Joe's agreement to communicate electronically for purposes outside the scope of the business indicated by use of the business card.

C. Sally may have several e mail addresses - home, main office, office of a non-profit organization on whose board Sally sits. In each case, it may be reasonable to infer that Sally is willing to communicate electronically with respect to business related to the business/purpose associated with the respective e mail addresses. However, depending on the circumstances, it may not be reasonable to communicate with Sally for purposes other than those related to the purpose for which she maintained a particular e mail account.

D. Among the circumstances to be considered in finding an agreement would be the time when the assent occurred relative to the timing of the use of electronic communications. If one orders books from an on-line vendor, such as Bookseller.com, the intention to conduct that transaction and to receive any correspondence related to the transaction electronically can be inferred from the conduct. Accordingly, as to information related to that transaction it is reasonable for Bookseller to deal with the individual electronically.

## SECTION 7. LEGAL RECOGNITION OF ELECTRONIC RECORDS, ELECTRONIC SIGNATURES, AND ELECTRONIC CONTRACTS.

(a) A record or signature may not be denied legal effect or enforceability solely because it is in electronic form.

(b) A contract may not be denied legal effect or enforceability solely because an electronic record was used in its formation.

(c) If a law requires a record to be in writing, an electronic record satisfies the law.

(d) If a law requires a signature, an electronic signature satisfies the law.

Comment

Illustration 1: A sends the following e mail to B: "I hereby offer to buy widgets from you, delivery next Tuesday. /s/ A." B responds with the following e mail: "I accept your offer to buy widgets for delivery next Tuesday. /s/ B." The e mails may not be denied effect solely because they are electronic. In addition, the e mails do qualify as records under the Statute of Frauds. However, because there is no quantity stated in either record, the parties' agreement would be unenforceable under existing UCC Section 2 201(1).

Illustration 2: A sends the following e mail to B: "I hereby offer to buy 100 widgets for $1000, delivery next Tuesday. /s/ A." B responds with the following e mail: "I accept your offer to purchase 100 widgets for $1000, delivery next Tuesday. /s/ B." In this case the analysis is the same as in Illustration 1 except that here the records otherwise satisfy the requirements of UCC Section 2 201(1). The transaction may not be denied legal effect solely because there is not a pen and ink "writing" or "signature".

## SECTION 8. PROVISION OF INFORMATION IN WRITING; PRESENTATION OF RECORDS.

(a) If parties have agreed to conduct a transaction by electronic means and a law requires a person to provide, send, or deliver information in writing to another person, the requirement is satisfied if the information is provided, sent, or delivered, as the case may be, in an electronic record capable of retention by the recipient at the time of receipt. An electronic record is not capable of retention by the recipient if the sender or its information processing system inhibits the ability of the recipient to print or store the electronic record.

## SECTION 9. ATTRIBUTION AND EFFECT OF ELECTRONIC RECORD AND ELECTRONIC SIGNATURE.

(a) An electronic record or electronic signature is attributable to a person if it was the act of the person. The act of the person may be shown in any manner, including a showing of the efficacy of any security procedure applied to determine the person to which the electronic record or electronic signature was attributable.

(b) The effect of an electronic record or electronic signature attributed to a person under subsection (a) is determined from the context and surrounding circumstances at the time of its creation, execution, or adoption, including the parties' agreement, if any, and otherwise as provided by law.

Comment

1. *** Although the rule may appear to state the obvious, it assures that the record or signature is not ascribed to a machine, as opposed to the person operating or program[m]ing the machine.

In each of the following cases, both the electronic record and electronic signature would be attributable to a person under subsection (a):

> A. The person types his/her name as part of an e mail purchase order;
>
> B. The person's employee, pursuant to authority, types the person's name as part of an e mail purchase order;
>
> C. The person's computer, programmed to order goods upon receipt of inventory information within particular parameters, issues a purchase order which includes the person's name, or other identifying information, as part of the order. ***

5. This section does apply in determining the effect of a "click-through" transaction. A "click-through" transaction involves a process which, if executed with an intent to "sign," will be an electronic signature. See definition of Electronic Signature. In the context of an anonymous "click-through," issues of proof will be paramount. This section will be relevant to establish that the resulting electronic record is attributable to a particular person upon the requisite proof, including security procedures which may track the source of the click-through.

SECTION 14. AUTOMATED TRANSACTION. In an automated transaction, the following rules apply:

(1) A contract may be formed by the interaction of electronic agents of the parties, even if no individual was aware of or reviewed the electronic agents' actions or the resulting terms and agreements.

(2) A contract may be formed by the interaction of an electronic agent and an individual, acting on the individual's own behalf or for another person, including by an interaction in which the individual performs actions that the individual is free to refuse to perform and which the individual knows or has reason to know will cause the electronic agent to complete the transaction or performance.

Comment

2. The process in paragraph (2) validates an anonymous click-through transaction. ***

For example, A goes to a website and is confronted by an initial screen which advises her that the information at this site is proprietary, that A may use the information for her own personal purposes, but that, by clicking below, A agrees that any other use without the site owner's permission is prohibited. If A clicks "agree" and downloads the information and then uses the information for other, prohibited purposes, should not A be bound by the click? It seems the answer properly should be, and would be, yes.

If the owner can show that the only way A could have obtained the information was from his website, and that the process to access the subject information required that A must have clicked the "I agree" button after having the ability to see the conditions on use, A has performed actions which A was free to refuse, which A knew would cause the site to grant her access, i.e., "complete the transaction." The terms of the resulting contract will be determined under general contract principles, but will include the limitation on A's use of the information, as a condition precedent to granting her access to the information.

3. In the transaction set forth in Comment 2, the record of the transaction also will include an electronic signature. By clicking "I agree" A adopted a process with the intent to "sign," i.e., bind herself to a legal obligation, the resulting record of the transaction. If a "signed writing" were required under otherwise applicable law, this transaction would be enforceable. If a "signed writing" were not required, it may be sufficient to establish that the electronic record is attributable to A under Section 9. Attribution may be shown in any manner reasonable including showing that, of necessity, A could only have gotten the information through the process at the website.

## SECTION 15. TIME AND PLACE OF SENDING AND RECEIPT.

(a) Unless otherwise agreed between the sender and the recipient, an electronic record is sent when it:

> (1) is addressed properly or otherwise directed properly to an information processing system that the recipient has designated or uses for the purpose of receiving electronic records or information of the type sent and from which the recipient is able to retrieve the electronic record;

> (2) is in a form capable of being processed by that system; and

> (3) enters an information processing system outside the control of the sender or of a person that sent the electronic record on behalf of the sender or enters a region of the information processing system designated or used by the recipient which is under the control of the recipient.

(b) Unless otherwise agreed between a sender and the recipient, an electronic record is received when:

> (1) it enters an information processing system that the recipient has designated or uses for the purpose of receiving electronic records or information of the type sent and from which the recipient is able to retrieve the electronic record; and

> (2) it is in a form capable of being processed by that system. \*\*\*

(e) An electronic record is received under subsection (b) even if no individual is aware of its receipt.

(f) Receipt of an electronic acknowledgment from an information processing system described in subsection (b) establishes that a record was received but, by itself, does not establish that the content sent corresponds to the content received. \*\*\*

Editorial Note

1. "Bomb-Shelters" Against UCITA

Two states, Maryland and Virginia, have adopted the Uniform Computer Information Transaction Act (UCITA), with some modifications. However, UCITA proved unpopular, and even its sponsor, NCCUSL, withdrew support. Iowa, North Carolina, Vermont, and West Virginia have each adopted "bomb-shelter" provisions that forbid application of other states' UCITA rules. The Iowa statute is typical: "A choice of law provision in a computer information agreement which provides that the contract is to be interpreted pursuant to the laws of a state that has enacted the uniform computer information transactions Act, as proposed by the national conference of commissioners on uniform state laws, or any substantially similar law, is voidable and the agreement shall be interpreted pursuant to the laws of this state if the party against whom enforcement of the choice of law provision is sought is a resident of this state or has its principal place of business located in this state." IOWA CODE ANN. § 554D.104 (West 2001 & Supp. 2002).

# Taxation

# INTERNET TAX FREEDOM ACT (1998)

Originally passed Oct. 21, 1998, Amended 2007

§ 1101. Moratorium

(a) Moratorium No State or political subdivision thereof shall impose any of the following taxes:

(1) Taxes on Internet access.

(2) Multiple or discriminatory taxes on electronic commerce.

(b) Preservation of state and local taxing authority. Except as provided in this section, nothing in this title [this note] shall be construed to modify, impair, or supersede, or authorize the modification, impairment, or superseding of, any State or local law pertaining to taxation that is otherwise permissible by or under the Constitution of the United States or other Federal law and in effect on the date of enactment of this Act [Oct. 21, 1998].

***

(3) Definitions. In this subsection:

(A) By means of the World Wide Web. The term 'by means of the World Wide Web' means by placement of material in a computer server-based file archive so that it is publicly accessible, over the Internet, using hypertext transfer protocol, file transfer protocol, or other similar protocols.

(B) Commercial purposes; engaged in the business.

(i) Commercial purposes. A person shall be considered to make a communication for commercial purposes only if such person is engaged in the business of making such communications.

(ii) Engaged in the business. The term 'engaged in the business' means that the person who makes a communication, or offers to make a communication, by means of the World Wide Web, that includes any material that is harmful to minors, devotes time, attention, or labor to such activities, as a regular course of such person's trade or business, with the objective of earning a profit as a result of such activities (although it is not necessary that the person make a profit or that the making or offering to make such communications be the person's sole or principal business or source of income). A person may be considered to be engaged in the business of making, by means of the World Wide Web, communications for commercial purposes that include material that is harmful to minors, only if the person knowingly causes the material that is harmful to minors to be posted on the World Wide Web or knowingly solicits such material to be posted on the World Wide Web.

(C) Internet. The term 'Internet' means collectively the myriad of computer and telecommunications facilities, including equipment and operating software, which comprise the interconnected world-wide network of networks that employ the Transmission Control

Protocol/Internet Protocol, or any predecessor or successor protocols to such protocol, to communicate information of all kinds by wire or radio.

(D) Internet access service. The term 'Internet access service' means a service that enables users to access content, information, electronic mail, or other services offered over the Internet and may also include access to proprietary content, information, and other services as part of a package of services offered to consumers. The term 'Internet access service' does not include telecommunications services, except to the extent such services are purchased, used, or sold by a provider of Internet access to provide Internet access.

(E) Internet information location tool. The term 'Internet information location tool' means a service that refers or links users to an online location on the World Wide Web. Such term includes directories, indices, references, pointers, and hypertext links.

(F) Material that is harmful to minors. The term 'material that is harmful to minors' means any communication, picture, image, graphic image file, article, recording, writing, or other matter of any kind that is obscene or that

> (i)the average person, applying contemporary community standards, would find, taking the material as a whole and with respect to minors, is designed to appeal to, or is designed to pander to, the prurient interest;

> (ii)depicts, describes, or represents, in a manner patently offensive with respect to minors, an actual or simulated sexual act or sexual contact, an actual or simulated normal or perverted sexual act, or a lewd exhibition of the genitals or post-pubescent female breast; and

> (iii)taken as a whole, lacks serious literary, artistic, political, or scientific value for minors.

(G) Minor. The term 'minor' means any person under 17 years of age.

(H) Telecommunications carrier; telecommunications service. The terms 'telecommunications carrier' and 'telecommunications service' have the meanings given such terms in section 3 of the Communications Act of 1934 (47 U.S.C. 153).

(e) Additional exception to moratorium.

(1) In general. Subsection (a) shall also not apply with respect to an Internet access provider, unless, at the time of entering into an agreement with a customer for the provision of Internet access services, such provider offers such customer (either for a fee or at no charge) screening software that is designed to permit the customer to limit access to material on the Internet that is harmful to minors.

(2) Definitions. In this subsection:

(A) Internet access provider. The term 'Internet access provider' means a person engaged in the business of providing a computer and communications facility through which a customer may obtain access to the Internet, but does not include a common carrier to the extent that it provides only telecommunications services.

(B) Internet access services. The term 'Internet access services' means the provision of computer and communications services through which a customer using a computer and a modem or other communications device may obtain access to the Internet, but does not include telecommunications services provided by a common carrier.

(C) Screening software. The term 'screening software' means software that is designed to permit a person to limit access to material on the Internet that is harmful to minors.

(3) Applicability. Paragraph (1) shall apply to agreements for the provision of Internet access services entered into on or after the date that is 6 months after the date of enactment of this Act [Oct. 21, 1998].

***

Sec. 1104. Grandfathering of states that tax Internet access

(a) Pre-October 1998 taxes.

(1) In general. Section 1101(a) [of this note] does not apply to a tax on Internet access that was generally imposed and actually enforced prior to October 1, 1998, if, before that date

(A) the tax was authorized by statute; and

(B) Either

(i) a provider of Internet access services had a reasonable opportunity to know, by virtue of a rule or other public proclamation made by the appropriate administrative agency of the State or political subdivision thereof, that such agency has interpreted and applied such tax to Internet access services; or

(ii) a State or political subdivision thereof generally collected such tax on charges for Internet access.

(2) Termination.

(A) In general. Except as provided in subparagraph (B), this subsection shall not apply after June 30, 2020.

(B) State telecommunications service tax.

(i) Date for termination. This subsection shall not apply after November 1, 2006, with respect to a State telecommunications service tax described in clause (ii).

(ii) Description of tax. A State telecommunications service tax referred to in subclause (i) is a State tax

(I) enacted by State law on or after October 1, 1991, and imposing a tax on telecommunications service; and

(II) applied to Internet access through administrative code or regulation issued on or after December 1, 2002.

(3) Exception. Paragraphs (1) and (2) shall not apply to any State that has, more than 24 months prior to the date of enactment of this paragraph [Oct. 31, 2007], enacted legislation to repeal the State's taxes on

Internet access or issued a rule or other proclamation made by the appropriate agency of the State that such State agency has decided to no longer apply such tax to Internet access.

(b) Pre-November 2003 taxes.

> (1) In general. Section 1101(a) [of this note] does not apply to a tax on Internet access that was generally imposed and actually enforced as of November 1, 2003, if, as of that date, the tax was authorized by statute and
>
>> (A) a provider of Internet access services had a reasonable opportunity to know by virtue of a public rule or other public proclamation made by the appropriate administrative agency of the State or political subdivision thereof, that such agency has interpreted and applied such tax to Internet access services; and
>>
>> (B) a State or political subdivision thereof generally collected such tax on charges for Internet access.
>
> (2) Termination. This subsection shall not apply after November 1, 2005.

(c) Application of definition.

> (1) In general. Effective as of November 1, 2003
>
>> (A) for purposes of subsection (a), the term 'Internet access' shall have the meaning given such term by section 1104(5) of this Act [of this note], as enacted on October 21, 1998; and
>>
>> (B) for purposes of subsection (b), the term 'Internet access' shall have the meaning given such term by section 1104(5) of this Act [of this note] as enacted on October 21, 1998, and amended by section 2(c) of the Internet Tax Nondiscrimination Act (Public Law 108-435).
>
> (2) Exceptions. Paragraph (1) shall not apply until June 30, 2008, to a tax on Internet access that is
>
>> (A) generally imposed and actually enforced on telecommunications service purchased, used, or sold by a provider of Internet access, but only if the appropriate administrative agency of a State or political subdivision thereof issued a public ruling prior to July 1, 2007, that applied such tax to such service in a manner that is inconsistent with paragraph (1); or
>>
>> (B) the subject of litigation instituted in a judicial court of competent jurisdiction prior to July 1, 2007, in which a State or political subdivision is seeking to enforce, in a manner that is inconsistent with paragraph (1), such tax on telecommunications service purchased, used, or sold by a provider of Internet access.
>
> (3) No inference. No inference of legislative construction shall be drawn from this subsection or the amendments to section 1105(5) [of this note] made by the Internet Tax Freedom Act Amendments Act of 2007 [Pub.L. 110-108, Oct. 31, 2007, 121 Stat. 1024] for any period prior to June 30, 2008, with respect to any tax subject to the exceptions described in subparagraphs (A) and (B) of paragraph (2).

§ 1105. Definitions

For the purposes of this title [this note]:

(1) Bit tax. The term 'bit tax' means any tax on electronic commerce expressly imposed on or measured by the volume of digital information transmitted electronically, or the volume of digital information per unit of time transmitted electronically, but does not include taxes imposed on the provision of telecommunications.

(2) Discriminatory tax. The term 'discriminatory tax' means

(A) any tax imposed by a State or political subdivision thereof on electronic commerce that

(i) is not generally imposed and legally collectible by such State or such political subdivision on transactions involving similar property, goods, services, or information accomplished through other means;

(ii) is not generally imposed and legally collectible at the same rate by such State or such political subdivision on transactions involving similar property, goods, services, or information accomplished through other means, unless the rate is lower as part of a phase-out of the tax over not more than a 5-year period;

(iii) imposes an obligation to collect or pay the tax on a different person or entity than in the case of transactions involving similar property, goods, services, or information accomplished through other means;

(iv) establishes a classification of Internet access service providers or online service providers for purposes of establishing a higher tax rate to be imposed on such providers than the tax rate generally applied to providers of similar information services delivered through other means; or

(B) any tax imposed by a State or political subdivision thereof, if

(i) the sole ability to access a site on a remote seller's out-of-State computer server is considered a factor in determining a remote seller's tax collection obligation; or

(ii) a provider of Internet access service or online services is deemed to be the agent of a remote seller for determining tax collection obligations solely as a result of

(I) the display of a remote seller's information or content on the out-of-State computer server of a provider of Internet access service or online services; or

(II) the processing of orders through the out-of-State computer server of a provider of Internet access service or online services.

(3) Electronic commerce. The term 'electronic commerce' means any transaction conducted over the Internet or through Internet access, comprising the sale, lease, license, offer, or delivery of property, goods, services, or information, whether or not for consideration, and includes the provision of Internet access.

(4) Internet. The term 'Internet' means collectively the myriad of computer and telecommunications facilities, including equipment and operating software, which comprise the interconnected world-wide network of networks that employ the Transmission Control Protocol/Internet Protocol, or any predecessor or successor protocols to such protocol, to communicate information of all kinds by wire or radio.

(5) Internet access. The term 'Internet access'

(A)means a service that enables users to connect to the Internet to access content, information, or other services offered over the Internet;

(B)includes the purchase, use or sale of telecommunications by a provider of a service described in subparagraph (A) to the extent such telecommunications are purchased, used or sold.

(i)to provide such service; or

(ii)to otherwise enable users to access content, information or other services offered over the Internet;

(C)includes services that are incidental to the provision of the service described in subparagraph (A) when furnished to users as part of such service, such as a home page, electronic mail and instant messaging (including voice- and video-capable electronic mail and instant messaging), video clips, and personal electronic storage capacity;

(D)does not include voice, audio or video programming, or other products and services (except services described in subparagraph (A), (B), (C), or (E)) that utilize Internet protocol or any successor protocol and for which there is a charge, regardless of whether such charge is separately stated or aggregated with the charge for services described in subparagraph (A), (B), (C), or (E); and

(E)includes a homepage, electronic mail and instant messaging (including voice- and video-capable electronic mail and instant messaging), video clips, and personal electronic storage capacity, that are provided independently or not packaged with Internet access.

(6) Multiple tax.

(A) In general. The term 'multiple tax' means any tax that is imposed by one State or political subdivision thereof on the same or essentially the same electronic commerce that is also subject to another tax imposed by another State or political subdivision thereof (whether or not at the same rate or on the same basis), without a credit (for example, a resale exemption certificate) for taxes paid in other jurisdictions.

(B) Exception. Such term shall not include a sales or use tax imposed by a State and 1 or more political subdivisions thereof on the same electronic commerce or a tax on persons engaged in electronic commerce which also may have been subject to a sales or use tax thereon.

(C) Sales or use tax. For purposes of subparagraph (B), the term 'sales or use tax' means a tax that is imposed on or incident to the sale, purchase, storage, consumption, distribution, or other use of tangible personal property or services as may be defined by laws imposing such tax and which is measured by the amount of the sales price or other charge for such property or service.

(7) State. The term 'State' means any of the several States, the District of Columbia, or any commonwealth, territory, or possession of the United States.

(8) Tax.

(A) In general. The term 'tax' means

(i)any charge imposed by any governmental entity for the purpose of generating revenues for governmental purposes, and is not a fee imposed for a specific privilege, service, or benefit conferred; or

(ii)the imposition on a seller of an obligation to collect and to remit to a governmental entity any sales or use tax imposed on a buyer by a governmental entity.

(B) Exception. Such term does not include any franchise fee or similar fee imposed by a State or local franchising authority, pursuant to section 622 or 653 of the Communications Act of 1934 (47 U.S.C. 542, 573), or any other fee related to obligations or telecommunications carriers under the Communications Act of 1934 (47 U.S.C. 151 et seq.).

(9) Telecommunications. The term 'telecommunications' means 'telecommunications' as such term is defined in section 3(43) of the Communications Act of 1934 (47 U.S.C. 153(43)) and 'telecommunications service' as such term is defined in section 3(46) of such Act (47 U.S.C. 153(46)), and includes communications services (as defined in section 4251 of the Internal Revenue Code of 1986 (26 U.S.C. 4251)).

(10) Tax on Internet access.

(A) In general. The term 'tax on Internet access' means a tax on Internet access, regardless of whether such tax is imposed on a provider of Internet access or a buyer of Internet access and regardless of the terminology used to describe the tax.

(B) General exception. The term 'tax on Internet access' does not include a tax levied upon or measured by net income, capital stock, net worth, or property value.

(C) Specific exception.

(i) Specified taxes. Effective November 1, 2007, the term 'tax on Internet access' also does not include a State tax expressly levied on commercial activity, modified gross receipts, taxable margin, or gross income of the business, by a State law specifically using one of the foregoing terms, that

(I)was enacted after June 20, 2005, and before November 1, 2007 (or, in the case of a State business and occupation tax, was enacted after January 1, 1932, and before January 1, 1936);

(II)replaced, in whole or in part, a modified value-added tax or a tax levied upon or measured by net income, capital stock, or net worth (or, is a State business and occupation tax that was enacted after January 1, 1932 and before January 1, 1936);

(III)is imposed on a broad range of business activity; and

(IV)is not discriminatory in its application to providers of communication services, Internet access, or telecommunications.

(ii) Modifications. Nothing in this subparagraph shall be construed as a limitation on a State's ability to make modifications to a tax covered by clause (i) of this subparagraph after November 1, 2007, as long as the modifications do not substantially narrow the range of business activities on which the tax is imposed or otherwise disqualify the tax under clause (i).

(iii) No inference. No inference of legislative construction shall be drawn from this subparagraph regarding the application of subparagraph (A) or (B) to any tax described in clause (i) for periods prior to November 1, 2007.

# Domain Names

## ICANN Uniform Domain Name Dispute Resolution Policy (1999)

1. Purpose.

This Uniform Domain Name Dispute Resolution Policy (the "Policy") has been adopted by the Internet Corporation for Assigned Names and Numbers ("ICANN"), is incorporated by reference into your Registration Agreement, and sets forth the terms and conditions in connection with a dispute between you and any party other than us (the registrar) over the registration and use of an Internet domain name registered by you. Proceedings under Paragraph 4 of this Policy will be conducted according to the Rules for Uniform Domain Name Dispute Resolution Policy (the "Rules of Procedure"), which are available at www.icann.org/udrp/udrp-rules-24oct99.htm, and the selected administrative-dispute-resolution service provider's supplemental rules.

2. Your Representations.

By applying to register a domain name, or by asking us to maintain or renew a domain name registration, you hereby represent and warrant to us that (a) the statements that you made in your Registration Agreement are complete and accurate; (b) to your knowledge, the registration of the domain name will not infringe upon or otherwise violate the rights of any third party; (c) you are not registering the domain name for an unlawful purpose; and (d) you will not knowingly use the domain name in violation of any applicable laws or regulations. It is your responsibility to determine whether your domain name registration infringes or violates someone else's rights.

3. Cancellations, Transfers, and Changes.

We will cancel, transfer or otherwise make changes to domain name registrations under the following circumstances:

> a. subject to the provisions of Paragraph 8, our receipt of written or appropriate electronic instructions from you or your authorized agent to take such action;

> b. our receipt of an order from a court or arbitral tribunal, in each case of competent jurisdiction, requiring such action; and/or

> c. our receipt of a decision of an Administrative Panel requiring such action in any administrative proceeding to which you were a party and which was conducted under this Policy or a later version of this Policy adopted by ICANN. (See Paragraph 4(i) and (k) below.)

We may also cancel, transfer or otherwise make changes to a domain name registration in accordance with the terms of your Registration Agreement or other legal requirements.

4. Mandatory Administrative Proceeding.

This Paragraph sets forth the type of disputes for which you are required to submit to a mandatory administrative proceeding. These proceedings will be conducted before one of the administrative-dispute-resolution service providers listed at www.icann.org/udrp/approved-providers.htm (each, a "Provider").

a. Applicable Disputes. You are required to submit to a mandatory administrative proceeding in the event that a third party (a "complainant") asserts to the applicable Provider, in compliance with the Rules of Procedure, that

(i) your domain name is identical or confusingly similar to a trademark or service mark in which the complainant has rights; and

(ii) you have no rights or legitimate interests in respect of the domain name; and

(iii) your domain name has been registered and is being used in bad faith.

In the administrative proceeding, the complainant must prove that each of these three elements are present.

b. Evidence of Registration and Use in Bad Faith. For the purposes of Paragraph 4(a)(iii), the following circumstances, in particular but without limitation, if found by the Panel to be present, shall be evidence of the registration and use of a domain name in bad faith:

(i) circumstances indicating that you have registered or you have acquired the domain name primarily for the purpose of selling, renting, or otherwise transferring the domain name registration to the complainant who is the owner of the trademark or service mark or to a competitor of that complainant, for valuable consideration in excess of your documented out-of-pocket costs directly related to the domain name; or

(ii) you have registered the domain name in order to prevent the owner of the trademark or service mark from reflecting the mark in a corresponding domain name, provided that you have engaged in a pattern of such conduct; or

(iii) you have registered the domain name primarily for the purpose of disrupting the business of a competitor; or

(iv) by using the domain name, you have intentionally attempted to attract, for commercial gain, Internet users to your web site or other on-line location, by creating a likelihood of confusion with the complainant's mark as to the source, sponsorship, affiliation, or endorsement of your web site or location or of a product or service on your web site or location.

c. How to Demonstrate Your Rights to and Legitimate Interests in the Domain Name in Responding to a Complaint. When you receive a complaint, you should refer to Paragraph 5 of the Rules of Procedure in determining how your response should be prepared. Any of the following circumstances, in particular but without limitation, if found by the Panel to be proved based on its evaluation of all evidence presented, shall demonstrate your rights or legitimate interests to the domain name for purposes of Paragraph 4(a)(ii):

(i) before any notice to you of the dispute, your use of, or demonstrable preparations to use, the domain name or a name corresponding to the domain name in connection with a bona fide offering of goods or services; or

(ii) you (as an individual, business, or other organization) have been commonly known by the domain name, even if you have acquired no trademark or service mark rights; or

(iii) you are making a legitimate noncommercial or fair use of the domain name, without intent for commercial gain to misleadingly divert consumers or to tarnish the trademark or service mark at issue.

d. Selection of Provider. The complainant shall select the Provider from among those approved by ICANN by submitting the complaint to that Provider. The selected Provider will administer the proceeding, except in cases of consolidation as described in Paragraph 4(f).

e. Initiation of Proceeding and Process and Appointment of Administrative Panel. The Rules of Procedure state the process for initiating and conducting a proceeding and for appointing the panel that will decide the dispute (the "Administrative Panel").

f. Consolidation. In the event of multiple disputes between you and a complainant, either you or the complainant may petition to consolidate the disputes before a single Administrative Panel. This petition shall be made to the first Administrative Panel appointed to hear a pending dispute between the parties. This Administrative Panel may consolidate before it any or all such disputes in its sole discretion, provided that the disputes being consolidated are governed by this Policy or a later version of this Policy adopted by ICANN.

g. Fees. All fees charged by a Provider in connection with any dispute before an Administrative Panel pursuant to this Policy shall be paid by the complainant, except in cases where you elect to expand the Administrative Panel from one to three panelists as provided in Paragraph 5(b)(iv) of the Rules of Procedure, in which case all fees will be split evenly by you and the complainant.

h. Our Involvement in Administrative Proceedings. We do not, and will not, participate in the administration or conduct of any proceeding before an Administrative Panel. In addition, we will not be liable as a result of any decisions rendered by the Administrative Panel.

i. Remedies. The remedies available to a complainant pursuant to any proceeding before an Administrative Panel shall be limited to requiring the cancellation of your domain name or the transfer of your domain name registration to the complainant.

j. Notification and Publication. The Provider shall notify us of any decision made by an Administrative Panel with respect to a domain name you have registered with us. All decisions under this Policy will be published in full over the Internet, except when an Administrative Panel determines in an exceptional case to redact portions of its decision.

k. Availability of Court Proceedings. The mandatory administrative proceeding requirements set forth in Paragraph 4 shall not prevent either you or the complainant from submitting the dispute to a court of competent jurisdiction for independent resolution before such mandatory administrative proceeding is commenced or after such proceeding is concluded. If an Administrative Panel decides that your domain name registration should be canceled or transferred, we will wait ten (10) business days (as observed in the location of our principal office) after we are informed by the applicable Provider of the Administrative Panel's decision before implementing that decision. We will then implement the decision unless we have received from you during that ten (10) business day period official documentation (such as a copy of a complaint, file-stamped by the clerk of the court) that you have commenced a lawsuit against the complainant in a jurisdiction to which the complainant has submitted under Paragraph 3(b)(xiii) of the Rules of Procedure. (In general, that jurisdiction is either the location of our principal office or of your address as shown in our Whois database. See Paragraphs 1 and 3(b)(xiii) of the Rules of Procedure for details.) If we receive such documentation within the ten (10) business day period, we will not implement the Administrative Panel's decision, and we will take no further action, until we receive (i) evidence satisfactory to us of a resolution between the parties; (ii) evidence satisfactory to us that your lawsuit has been dismissed or withdrawn; or (iii) a copy of an order from such court dismissing your lawsuit or ordering that you do not have the right to continue to use your domain name.

5. All Other Disputes and Litigation.

All other disputes between you and any party other than us regarding your domain name registration that are not brought pursuant to the mandatory administrative proceeding provisions of Paragraph 4 shall be resolved between you and such other party through any court, arbitration or other proceeding that may be available.

6. Our Involvement in Disputes.

We will not participate in any way in any dispute between you and any party other than us regarding the registration and use of your domain name. You shall not name us as a party or otherwise include us in any such proceeding. In the event that we are named as a party in any such proceeding, we reserve the right to raise any and all defenses deemed appropriate, and to take any other action necessary to defend ourselves.

7. Maintaining the Status Quo.

We will not cancel, transfer, activate, deactivate, or otherwise change the status of any domain name registration under this Policy except as provided in Paragraph 3 above.

8. Transfers During a Dispute.

a. Transfers of a Domain Name to a New Holder. You may not transfer your domain name registration to another holder (i) during a pending administrative proceeding brought pursuant to Paragraph 4 or for a period of fifteen (15) business days (as observed in the location of our principal place of business) after such proceeding is concluded; or (ii) during a pending court proceeding or arbitration commenced regarding your domain name unless the party to whom the domain name registration is being transferred agrees, in writing, to be bound by the decision of the court or arbitrator. We reserve the right to cancel any transfer of a domain name registration to another holder that is made in violation of this subparagraph.

b. Changing Registrars. You may not transfer your domain name registration to another registrar during a pending administrative proceeding brought pursuant to Paragraph 4 or for a period of fifteen (15) business days (as observed in the location of our principal place of business) after such proceeding is concluded. You may transfer administration of your domain name registration to another registrar during a pending court action or arbitration, provided that the domain name you have registered with us shall continue to be subject to the proceedings commenced against you in accordance with the terms of this Policy. In the event that you transfer a domain name registration to us during the pendency of a court action or arbitration, such dispute shall remain subject to the domain name dispute policy of the registrar from which the domain name registration was transferred.

9. Policy Modifications.

We reserve the right to modify this Policy at any time with the permission of ICANN. We will post our revised Policy at <URL> at least thirty (30) calendar days before it becomes effective. Unless this Policy has already been invoked by the submission of a complaint to a Provider, in which event the version of the Policy in effect at the time it was invoked will apply to you until the dispute is over, all such changes will be binding upon you with respect to any domain name registration dispute, whether the dispute arose before, on or after the effective date of our change. In the event that you object to a change in this Policy, your sole remedy is to cancel your domain name registration with us, provided that you will not be entitled to a refund of any fees you paid to us. The revised Policy will apply to you until you cancel your domain name registration.

# ANTICYBERSQUATTING CONSUMER PROTECTION ACT
## *15 USC § 1125 et seq.*
### (Nov. 29, 1999)

15 USC § 1125

(d) Cyberpiracy Prevention

    (1)    (A) A person shall be liable in a civil action by the owner of a mark, including a personal name which is protected as a mark under this section, if, without regard to the goods or services of the parties, that person

        (i) has a bad faith intent to profit from that mark, including a personal name which is protected as a mark under this section; and

        (ii) registers, traffics in, or uses a domain name that

            (I) in the case of a mark that is distinctive at the time of registration of the domain name, is identical or confusingly similar to that mark;

            (II) in the case of a famous mark that is famous at the time of registration of the domain name, is identical or confusingly similar to or dilutive of that mark; or

            (III) is a trademark, word, or name protected by reason of section 706 of title 18, United States Code, or section 220506 of title 36, United States Code.

    (B)    (i) In determining whether a person has a bad faith intent described under subparagraph (A), a court may consider factors such as, but not limited to

        (I) the trademark or other intellectual property rights of the person, if any, in the domain name;

        (II) the extent to which the domain name consists of the legal name of the person or a name that is otherwise commonly used to identify that person;

        (III) the person's prior use, if any, of the domain name in connection with the bona fide offering of any goods or services;

        (IV) the person's bona fide noncommercial or fair use of the mark in a site accessible under the domain name;

        (V) the person's intent to divert consumers from the mark owner's online location to a site accessible under the domain name that could harm the goodwill represented by the mark, either for commercial gain or with the intent to tarnish or disparage the mark, by creating a likelihood of confusion as to the source, sponsorship, affiliation, or endorsement of the site;

(VI) the person's offer to transfer, sell, or otherwise assign the domain name to the mark owner or any third party for financial gain without having used, or having an intent to use, the domain name in the bona fide offering of any goods or services, or the person's prior conduct indicating a pattern of such conduct;

(VII) the person's provision of material and misleading false contact information when applying for the registration of the domain name, the person's intentional failure to maintain accurate contact information, or the person's prior conduct indicating a pattern of such conduct;

(VIII) the person's registration or acquisition of multiple domain names which the person knows are identical or confusingly similar to marks of others that are distinctive at the time of registration of such domain names, or dilutive of famous marks of others that are famous at the time of registration of such domain names, without regard to the goods or services of the parties; and

(IX) the extent to which the mark incorporated in the person's domain name registration is or is not distinctive and famous within the meaning of subsection (C)(1) of section 43.

(ii) Bad faith intent described under subparagraph (A) shall not be found in any case in which the court determines that the person believed and had reasonable grounds to believe that the use of the domain name was a fair use or otherwise lawful.

(C) In any civil action involving the registration, trafficking, or use of a domain name under this paragraph, a court may order the forfeiture or cancellation of the domain name or the transfer of the domain name to the owner of the mark.

(D) A person shall be liable for using a domain name under subparagraph (A) only if that person is the domain name registrant or that registrant's authorized licensee.

(E) As used in this paragraph, the term 'traffics in' refers to transactions that include, but are not limited to, sales, purchases, loans, pledges, licenses, exchanges of currency, and any other transfer for consideration or receipt in exchange for consideration.

(2) (A) The owner of a mark may file an in rem civil action against a domain name in the judicial district in which the domain name registrar, domain name registry, or other domain name authority that registered or assigned the domain name is located if

(i) the domain name violates any right of the owner of a mark registered in the Patent and Trademark Office, or protected under subsection (a) or (c); and

(ii) the court finds that the owner

(I) is not able to obtain in personam jurisdiction over a person who would have been a defendant in a civil action under paragraph (1); or

(II) through due diligence was not able to find a person who would have been a defendant in a civil action under paragraph (1) by

(aa) sending a notice of the alleged violation and intent to proceed under this paragraph to the registrant of the domain name at the postal and e-mail address provided by the registrant to the registrar; and

(bb) publishing notice of the action as the court may direct promptly after filing the action.

(B) The actions under subparagraph (A)(ii) shall constitute service of process.

(C) In an in rem action under this paragraph, a domain name shall be deemed to have its situs in the judicial district in which

(i) the domain name registrar, registry, or other domain name authority that registered or assigned the domain name is located; or

(ii) documents sufficient to establish control and authority regarding the disposition of the registration and use of the domain name are deposited with the court.

(D) (i) The remedies in an in rem action under this paragraph shall be limited to a court order for the forfeiture or cancellation of the domain name or the transfer of the domain name to the owner of the mark. Upon receipt of written notification of a filed, stamped copy of a complaint filed by the owner of a mark in a United States district court under this paragraph, the domain name registrar, domain name registry, or other domain name authority shall

(I) expeditiously deposit with the court documents sufficient to establish the court's control and authority regarding the disposition of the registration and use of the domain name to the court; and

(II) not transfer, suspend, or otherwise modify the domain name during the pendency of the action, except upon order of the court.

(ii) The domain name registrar or registry or other domain name authority shall not be liable for injunctive or monetary relief under this paragraph except in the case of bad faith or reckless disregard, which includes a willful failure to comply with any such court order.

(3) The civil action established under paragraph (1) and the in rem action established under paragraph (2), and any remedy available under either such action, shall be in addition to any other civil action or remedy otherwise applicable.

(4) The in rem jurisdiction established under paragraph (2) shall be in addition to any other jurisdiction that otherwise exists, whether in rem or in personam.".

## 15 USC § 1129

(b) CYBERPIRACY PROTECTIONS FOR INDIVIDUALS.

    (1) IN GENERAL.

        (A)    CIVIL LIABILITY. Any person who registers a domain name that consists of the name of another living person, or a name substantially and confusingly similar thereto, without that person's consent, with the specific intent to profit from such name by selling the domain name for financial gain to that person or any third party, shall be liable in a civil action by such person.

        (B)    EXCEPTION. A person who in good faith registers a domain name consisting of the name of another living person, or a name substantially and confusingly similar thereto, shall not be liable under this paragraph if such name is used in, affiliated with, or related to a work of authorship protected under title 17, United States Code, including a work made for hire as defined in section 101 of title 17, United States Code, and if the person registering the domain name is the copyright owner or licensee of the work, the person intends to sell the domain name in conjunction with the lawful exploitation of the work, and such registration is not prohibited by a contract between the registrant and the named person. The exception under this subparagraph shall apply only to a civil action brought under paragraph (1) and shall in no manner limit the protections afforded under the Trademark Act of 1946 (15 U.S.C. 1051 et seq.) or other provision of Federal or State law.

    (2)    REMEDIES. In any civil action brought under paragraph (1), a court may award injunctive relief, including the forfeiture or cancellation of the domain name or the transfer of the domain name to the plaintiff. The court may also, in its discretion, award costs and attorneys fees to the prevailing party.

    (3)    DEFINITION. In this subsection, the term "domain name" has the meaning given that term in section 45 of the Trademark Act of 1946 (15 U.S.C. 1127). \*\*\*

## 15 USC § 1114

(D)(v) A domain name registrant whose domain name has been suspended, disabled, or transferred under a policy described under clause (ii)(II) may, upon notice to the mark owner, file a civil action to establish that the registration or use of the domain name by such registrant is not unlawful under this Act. The court may grant injunctive relief to the domain name registrant, including the reactivation of the domain name or transfer of the domain name to the domain name registrant. \*\*\*

## 15 USCA § 1117

(b) STATUTORY DAMAGES. Section 35 of the Trademark Act of 1946 (15 U.S.C. 1117) is amended by adding at the end the following:

"(d) In a case involving a violation of section 43(d)(1), the plaintiff may elect, at any time before final judgment is rendered by the trial court, to recover, instead of actual damages and profits, an award of statutory damages in the amount of not less than $1,000 and not more than $100,000 per domain name, as the court considers just.